A SENIORS GUIDE TO THE S24 , S24+ AND S24 ULTRA

GETTING STARTED WITH THE 2024 SAMSUNG GALAXY

SCOTT LA COUNTE

RIDICULOUSLY
SIMPLE BOOKS

ANAHEIM, CALIFORNIA

www.RidiculouslySimpleBooks.com

Disclaimer: Please note, while every effort has been made to ensure accuracy, this book is not endorsed by Samsung, Inc. and should be considered unofficial.

Table of Contents

INTRODUCTION

Master Your Samsung Galaxy S24 and Its Innovative One UI 6.1

A seniors guide to the Galaxy S24's Rich Features

Embark on a journey of discovery with your new Samsung Galaxy S24, guided by this engaging and accessible book. Designed for both newcomers and seasoned Galaxy users, this guide is the perfect companion to help you unlock the full potential of your device without getting lost in technical jargon.

Dive into easy-to-follow instructions that cover everything from initial setup to mastering the camera, exploring the internet, and tweaking system settings. This guide is tailored to help you quickly learn and enjoy the most popular and powerful features of your S24. This book also delves into what sets the Galaxy S24 apart from other smartphones.

Inside, You'll Discover:

- The distinctive qualities of the Galaxy S24 compared to iOS, Android, and other smartphones.

- Simple steps to set up your new device.

- Making the most of your phone calls and app installations.

- Navigating accessibility features for an inclusive experience.
- Mastering the art of photography with the S24's advanced camera.
- Browsing the internet like a pro.
- Customizing system settings to suit your needs.
- You'll also learn how to use the best features on the latest OS: One UI 6.1
- And much more

Discover the wonders of your Samsung Galaxy S24 and its innovative One UI 6.1 - your journey to mastering this amazing device starts here!

Note: This guide is crafted with love by a Samsung enthusiasts and is not officially endorsed by Samsung.

[1]

Start Here

WHAT'S NEW TO ONE UI 6.1?

All Samsung devices are built off of Android OS, but they have their own branded UI on top of it called One UI. The latest is 6.1. One of the best things about the newest lineup of Galaxy phones? Samsung promises it will support them for at least seven years. That means you'll be getting all the latest updates for years to come.

What's new in One UI 6.1? Let's take a look at some of the biggest features.

Live Translate During Phone Calls
Imagine you're on a call with someone who speaks a different language. With the Galaxy S24,

language barriers are a thing of the past! The phone can translate what each person says in real-time. It's like having a personal interpreter in your pocket. This fantastic feature works on-device and supports 13 languages right from the start.

Chat Assist in Samsung Keyboard
Ever found yourself struggling to translate a message or needing to proofread a hastily typed email? The Samsung Keyboard now comes with built-in AI capabilities that can do all that and more. Whether you're emailing, posting on social media, or sending a quick text, this feature is your new best friend for clear and accurate communication in various languages.

Generative Photo Editing
Remember how Google wowed us with its Magic Editor? Samsung's generative photo editing is along the same lines. You can now tweak your photos by removing or moving objects, even tricky ones like reflections or shadows. The AI seamlessly reconstructs the background, making it look like the object was never there. It's like having a magic wand for your photos!

Transform Any Video to Slow Motion
Ever wished you could slow down a video to catch a special moment? With the Galaxy S24, any video in your gallery can be transformed into smooth slow motion with just a long press. The AI

fills in the gaps by generating extra frames, creating a seamless slow-motion effect as if the video was originally shot that way.

Circle to Search with Google

Here's something truly futuristic: if you see an image on your screen and want to know more about it, just hold down the home button and circle the item. Whether it's a landmark, an animal, or any random object, your phone will recognize it and pull up relevant Google Search results. It's like having a detective lens for the world around you.

Recorder Transcribe

Taking notes during long meetings can be tedious. But with the Galaxy S24, you can record the conversation and let the phone transcribe it for you. What's more, it can even summarize the recording into bullet points. This feature is a game-changer for professionals and students alike.

Note Assist for Samsung Notes

For those who love taking notes but find organizing them a hassle, the Note Assist feature on the Galaxy S24 Ultra is a blessing. It can sift through your notes, summarize them, and highlight key information. Plus, it creates predictive templates and organizes your notes based on how you use them. It's like having a personal assistant to keep your thoughts organized.

Android Auto Assists

Driving and staying connected can be challenging, but Android Auto assists make it a breeze. When your Galaxy S24 is in Android Auto mode, it smartly summarizes your chats and shows you the most crucial information at a glance. Quick-reply buttons, navigation setting, and ETA sharing features are all contextually offered based on your recent messages. It's about making your drive safer and more connected.

WHAT'S NEW TO ANDROID 14 OS

What about Android 14? What's new and exciting on that update–since Samsung is built on it. Let's take a quick peak.

Android 14 takes personalization to new heights. Ever wished for a more dynamic lock screen? Now you can jazz it up with cool new lock screen templates, a chic monochromatic theme, and even Ultra HDR images. And it doesn't stop there – create wallpapers with a unique parallax effect using your photos, turn your favorite emojis into cartoon-style backdrops, or explore the world of AI-generated wallpapers crafted from your own text prompts. It's all about making your phone uniquely yours!

Boosted Battery Life

Under the hood, Android 14 has been fine-tuned for even better efficiency, giving your phone's battery a much-needed boost. Thanks to smarter handling of background tasks and data transfers, your phone will last longer on a single charge. Plus, the handy "screen time since last full charge" feature is back, letting you keep an eye on your usage more easily.

Readability Redefined
For those who need larger fonts, Android 14 has got your back. You can now enlarge fonts up to 200%, and thanks to clever nonlinear scaling, your layout stays clean and clear, making it a boon for people with vision impairments.

Notification Innovations
Android 14 introduces camera and screen flashes for notifications – a feature that's as helpful as it is cool. Perfect for those with hearing difficulties or anyone who prefers a visual alert over sound or vibration. Customize the color of your display flash to suit your style!

Enhanced Hearing Aid Support
Good news for hearing aid users! Android 14 treats hearing aids not just as another Bluetooth device but gives them a dedicated space. Control where your sounds play – through your hearing aids or the phone's speakers. And if you love cranking up the volume, Android 14 will gently remind you to protect your ears.

More Control Over Your Photos and Videos

Android 14 respects your privacy. Choose exactly which photos and videos an app can access, rather than giving blanket permission. It's a thoughtful feature for those who value their digital privacy.

Stepping Up Security

In a move to outsmart malware, Android 14 blocks installations of outdated apps, keeping you safer. Enhanced support for biometric logins means more apps can ditch passwords in favor of more secure, biometric options.

PIN Protection Perfected

Keep your PIN safe and secret with Android 14. Disable the entry animation for an added layer of security, and if your PIN is six digits or more, it'll unlock instantly on the last digit – no more "OK" button.

Data Protection in the Digital Age

Android 14 is on guard, monitoring apps and games that might change their data sharing policies. It'll give you a heads-up if there's any change in how your data is being handled, keeping you informed and in control.

Tailor Your Regional Preferences

Whether it's the temperature unit, the first day of the week, or your preferred calendar style, Android 14 lets you set these preferences systemwide. They even stay put through backup and restore processes.

Navigating Made Intuitive
Navigating your phone is smoother than ever with Android 14's predictive back gestures and a new back arrow that complements your theme. Now, you'll always know where a swipe will take you.

Streamlined Sharing
The share menu gets a makeover in Android 14. Expect a more consistent experience across apps, with custom actions and intelligent suggestions making sharing quicker and more relevant.

[2]

THE OVERVIEW

FINDING YOUR WAY AROUND

People come to the Samsung from all sorts of different places: iPhone, other Android phone, flip phone, two Styrofoam cups tied together with string. This next section is a crash course in the interface. If you've used Android before, then it might seem a little simple, so skip ahead if you already know all of this.

If any of this seems a little rushed, there's good reason: it is! We'll cover these points in more detail later. This is just a quick starter / reference.

When you see your main screen for the first time, you will see six components. They are (from top to bottom): the Notification Bar, Add Weather Widget, Google Search App, Short Cuts Icons, Favorites Bar, navigation.

Notifications Bar - This is a pull-down menu (slide down to expand it) and it's where you'll see all your alerts (new email or text, for example) and where you can go to change settings quickly.

Add Weather Widget – Widgets are like mini apps that display information on your screen; weather is what's shown here, but they can be anything from Gmail, to calendars, and hundreds of things in between.

Google Search App – The Google Search app is another example of a widget. As the name implies, it can search Google for information; but it also searches apps on your phone.

Short Cuts Icons – These are apps that you frequently use and want quick access to.

Favorites Bar – These are like short cuts, except you see them on all your screens. You can add whatever you want to this area, but these are the apps Samsung thinks you'll use most.

Navigation Bar – These are shortcuts for getting around your phone: the first is the multi-task button, which helps you quickly switch apps; the next is the Home button which gets you back to the Home screen; and the last is the back button, which returns you to the previous screen.

So, what are these? Real quick, these are as follows:

Phone | Messages | Chrome Browser | Camera

- **Phone**: Do you want to take a wild guess what the phone button does? If you said brings you an ice cream, then maybe you aren't cut out for a phone. But if you said something along the lines of "It launches an app to call people" then you'll have no problem at all with your new device. Surprise, surprise: this pricey gadget that plays games, takes pictures, and keeps you up-to-date on political ramblings on social media does one more interesting thing: it calls people!
- **Message**: Message might be a little more open-ended than "Phone"; that could mean email message, text messages,

messages you keep getting on your bath-room mirror to put the toilet seat down. In this case, it means "text messages" (but really—put that toilet seat down...you aren't doing anyone any favors). This is the app you'll use whenever you want to text cute pictures of cats.

- **Chrome**: Whenever you want to surf the Internet, you'll use Chrome. There are actually several apps that do the same thing—like Firefox and Opera—but I recommend Chrome until you are comfortable with your phone. Personally, I think it's the best app for searching the Internet, but you'll soon learn that most things on the phone are about preference, and you may find another Internet browser that suits your needs better.

- **Camera**: This apps opens pictures of vintage cameras...just kidding! It's how you take pictures on your phone. You use this same app for videos as well.

NOTIFICATIONS BAR

Next to the short cut bar, the area you'll use the most is the notification bar. This is where you'll get, you guessed it, notifications! What's a notification? That's any kind of notice you have elected to receive. A few examples: text message alerts, email alerts, amber alerts, and apps that have updates.

When you drag your finger down from the notification bar, you'll get a list of several settings that you can adjust. Press and hold any of these options and you'll open an app with even more options.

From right to left these are the options you can change or use:

- Wi-fi
- Sound (tap to mute sounds)
- Bluetooth
- Lock the device from auto-rotating
- Airplane mode (which turns off wi-fi and Bluetooth)
- Flashlight

If you continue dragging down, this thin menu expands and there are a few more options.

The first is at the bottom of the screen—it's the slider, and it makes your device brighter or dimmer depending on which way you drag it.

Above that, there are several controls. Many of these controls are just an on / off toggle, but some let you long press to see expanded options. Some will be more obvious that others, but I'll go through each one quickly, starting from top left.

- Wi-Fi – Tap to turn off Wi-Fi; long press to change networks and see Wi-Fi set-tings.
- Sound – Tap to turn off sound; long press to see sound settings.

- Bluetooth – Turns off Bluetooth; long press to connect to a device or see Bluetooth settings.
- Autorotate – Tapping will lock the device orientation, so if you turn the device the screen will not rotate.
- Airplane mode – turns off features like Wi-Fi, cellular, and Bluetooth.
- Flashlight – Turns on the flash of your camera to let your phone act as a flashlight.
- Mobile Data – If you want to manually control if your phone is using mobile data or Wi-Fi, then you can toggle this on. There are a lot of reasons for this; sometimes you might find the Wi-Fi connection is too weak and you want to use mobile exclusively—but be careful: depending on what you are doing, mobile data can eat up your carriers data plan very quickly.
- Mobile hotspot – Toggling this on will let your phone act as a hotspot (so other devices can use your phone's Data connection to connect to the Internet); personally, I use this often to connect to my laptop on the go. Some carriers will charge extra for this service. You should also be careful, as this does go into data charges; if you let someone else share it and they decide to stream a movie, it's

going to eat up your data quick. Long pressing it will show you expanded settings.

- Power saving mode – turns on a power saving mode that will help your phone last longer; if you are low on batteries and not near a charger, this will help you get a little more life out of your phone. Long pressing it will bring up expanded power save features.
- Location – Toggling this on / off lets apps see your location; for example, if you are using a map for driving directions, it gives the app permission to see where you are located. Long pressing will show expanded location settings.
- Link to Windows – If you have a Windows computer, you can use this feature to send notifications to your linked Windows computer.
- Screen recorder – This option lets you create a video of what's on your screen; you can create a tutorial for something or even record a game. Long pressing will show expanded settings.

If you swipe you will see even more options to pick from.

- DeX – DeX turns your phone into a desktop experience when connected to an HDMI monitor.
- Smart view – lets you mirror your screen (or sound) to other devices (such as a Google Home).
- Nearby Share – Let's you share photos and documents with phones nearby you.
- Eye comfort shield – Toggling on will turn off the blue light on your phone; it gives your phone a more brownish hue. Looking at a blue light can make it difficult to sleep, so it's recommended to turn this on at night.
- Do not disturb – Turns off notifications so you don't receive messages or phone calls (they'll go straight to voice mail); long pressing expands Do not disturb settings.
- Dark mode – Gives menus and some apps a black background instead of white. Long pressing will show expanded settings.

Samsung got rid of a lot of options that they probably felt either weren't used or weren't use that often. But they're still there. On the last notification screen, tap the + icon and you'll see more options that you can add.

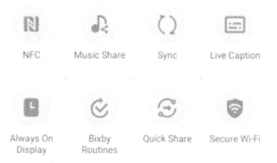

There are two screens of extra buttons (tap them and drag them to your notification bar to add them). The first screen shows:

- NFC – If you plan on putting credit cards on your phone to wirelessly pay for things at the checkout, make sure NFC is toggled on. Long pressing will show expanded settings.
- Music share – Shares music that you are listening to, so you can listen together. Long pressing will show expanded settings.
- Sync – Sync's your device across other devices.

- Live Captioning – This will be covered a little later, but toggling it on let's you add captions to your videos.
- Always on display – your display is always on when this is enabled. Long pressing will show expanded settings.
- Bixby routines – Sets up Bixby. Long pressing will show expanded settings.
- Quick share – This option lets you wirelessly share photos, videos and other files with another device. Long pressing will show expanded settings.
- Secure Wi-Fi – Creates a secure encryptions while using but public and personal wireless networks.

The next notification option screen has the following:

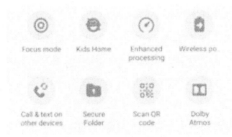

- Focus mode – Lets you set timers and turn off certain apps for a period of time to give you a more distraction-free experience. Long pressing will show expanded settings.

- Kids Home – Turns on kids mode, which gives your device a kid-friendly UI and turns off several apps.
- Enhanced Processioning – A mode that conserves battery by slowing your phone down.
- Wireless PowerShare – tapping this option lets you wirelessly power charge another wireless device (such as a watch or even another phone); your phone is essentially serving as a wireless charger to that other device. Long pressing it will bring up PowerShare settings.
- Call & text and other devices
- Secure folder – Creates a secure folder for your devices, so you can password protect certain apps and documents.
- Scan QR code – A QR code is sometimes seen on fliers; you can use this to scan it and see what the code links to.
- Dolby Amos – Toggling on will give your device superior Dolby Amos sound. Long pressing will show expanded settings.

On the notification area you'll also see two options for Media and Devices.

Media lets you control music and videos on other devices.

Devices lets you connect to devices using Bluetooth and see what devices you are already connected to.

Up on top is a handful of other controls.

The config button brings up expanded settings for notifications.

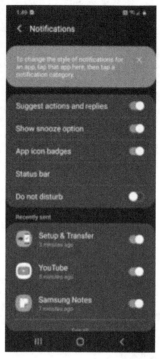

The power button will let you restart or power down your device.

GETTING AROUND QUICKLY

As mentioned, the bottom of the screen is your navigation area for getting around.

This is nice, but better is setting up gestures to handle navigating around your phone. This will turn this section off to give a tad more screen real estate.

To change it, swipe up from the bottom of your screen (this will bring up all your apps), then tap Settings. Next, go to the Display option.

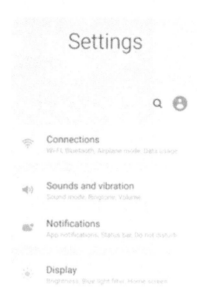

In Display options, scroll down until you get to Navigation bar, and then tap it.

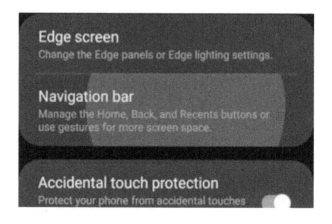

In the Navigation bar menu, select Full screen gestures.

Nice! It's gone! But what are the gestures?! Before you leave settings, it will give you a little preview of how they work, but below is a recap:

- Swipe up and release to get to your Home screen from any app.
- Swipe up and hold to bring up multitasking.

- Swipe right or left from the bottom edge of your screen to go backwards and forward.

You might recall that swiping up from the bottom showed you all your apps. That gesture now returns to the Home screen, so how do you see all your apps? From your Home screen, swipe up in the middle of the screen to see them.

When it comes to getting around your Samsung, learning how to use gestures will be the quickest, most effective method. You can change some of the gesture options by going to System > Gestures > System navigation.

The most important gesture is how to get back to the Home screen—there are no buttons after all. That's the easiest one to remember: swipe up from the bottom of the screen.

MULTITASKING

Those are the easy gestures to remember; if you want to move around quickly, however, you need to know the two big multitask gestures, which help you switch between apps.

The first is to see your open apps. To do this, swipe up like you're going to the Home screen, but keep going until about the middle of the screen and then stop and lift your finger—don't make a quick swipe-up gesture like you would when going Home. This will show you previews of all of your open apps, and you can swipe between them. Tap the one you want to open.

The quickest way to switch back and forth between two or three apps, however, is to swipe from left to right along the bottom edge of the screen. This swipes between apps in the order that you have used them.

ZOOM

Need to see text bigger? There are two ways to do that. Note: this works on many, but not all apps.

The first way is to pinch to zoom.

r with the Additic
: between you an
es. It is importan
Collectively, this l
s".

etween what the
al Terms say, ther
elation to that Se

The second way is to double tap on the text.

ROTATE

You probably have noticed if you rotate your phone, it rotates the screen. What if you don't want to rotate the entire screen? You can turn that off very easily. Swipe down and then tap the "arrows" button to enable or disable it.

EDGE BAR

One of the features that has always stood out on Samsung devices is the way they make use of all areas of your phone...right up to the edge.

The Edge bar brings up short cut menus quickly no matter where you are on the phone. To access it, swipe left from the side of your screen near the top; the Edge bar outline can just barely be seen on your Home screen. It's right next to the down volume button and extends just above the up volume button.

Swiping right brings up a side menu.

On the bottom left corner, you can click the bulleted list icon to see all of your Edge bar menus.

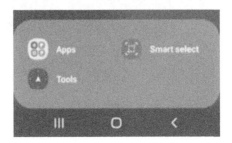

Swiping right and left lets you toggle between them.

Clicking on the config icon on the bottom left corner will let you select and deselect the Edge bar menus that are shown.

To add an app to the App Edge bar menu, just tap the + icon.

To remove an app, tap and hold the icon, then drag it to remove.

Smart select is a tool to create screenshots and GIFs (little animated images).

Rectangle captures a selected rectangle area of your screen.

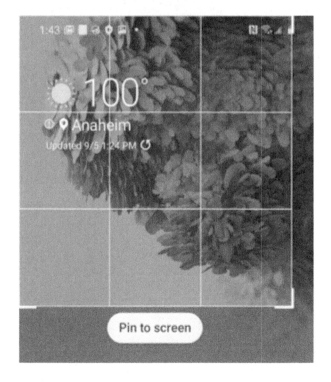

You can also go to somewhere like YouTube, where this tool would automatically locate the video and record it to create a GIF. Use the GIF capture icon to do this.

The oval tool will change the capture into a circular shape.

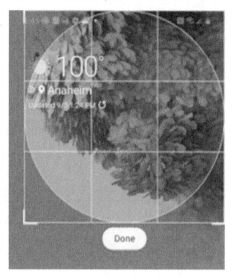

As the name implies, the Tools Edge bar, has a series of tools that you can use along with your phone. They help you take measurements, keep tallies, and use as a flashlight, or compass.

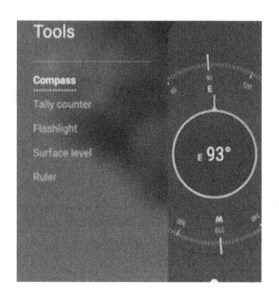

[3]

CUSTOMIZING THE PHONE

MAKING PRETTY SCREENS

If you've used an iPhone or iPad, then you may notice the screen looks a little...bare. There are only a few buttons on it. Maybe you like that. If so, then good for you! Skip ahead. If you want to decorate that screen with shortcuts and widgets, then read on.

ADDING SHORTCUTS

Any app you want on this screen, just find it and then press and hold; when a menu comes up, drag it upward until the screen appears and move it to where you want it to go.

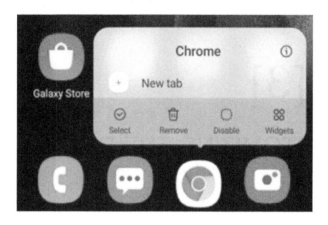

To remove an app from a screen, tap and hold, then tap Remove from the pop-up box.

WIDGETS

Shortcuts are nice, but widgets are better. Widgets are sort of like mini-programs that run on your screen. A common widget people put on their screen is the weather forecast. Throughout the day the widget will update automatically with up-to-date info.

It's such a popular widget that Samsung has put the option on your Home screen and you only have to tap it to set it up.

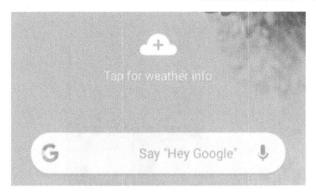

Once you add your city, it's going to automatically start showing. Clicking on it will open up the app.

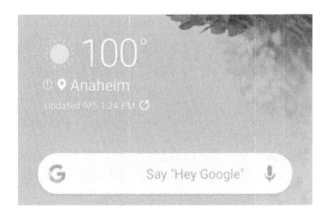

Weather is nice, but there are lots of widgets you can add to your Home screen. How do you get them?

There's actually a shortcut when you tap and hold over an app that has Widget capabilities (not all do).

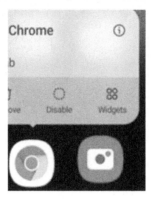

If you want to see all widgets available, then press and hold your finger on the middle of the screen. This brings up the Home screen options menu. Tap the Widgets icon.

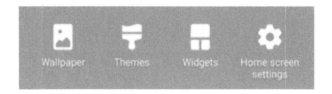

This will show you the most popular widgets, but if you know what you want, then just search for it.

For this example, I searched for Gmail, who I know has a widget. I tap it, then it let's me select where I want it on the screen.

When you tap on the widget, you'll notice little dots on the side. That lets you make it bigger or smaller. Just drag it to your ideal width and height.

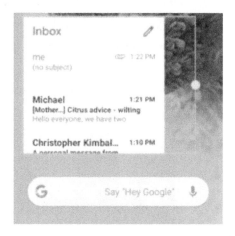

To remove any widget, just tap and hold it. From the pop-up, tap Remove from Home.

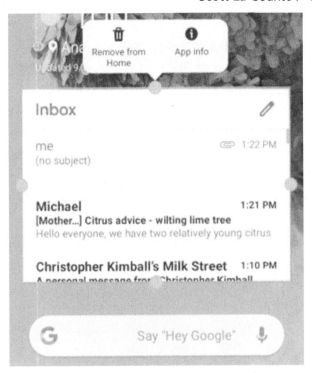

BATTERY WIDGET

If you have multiple Samsung devices (like the Galaxy Buds, S Pen, Galaxy Watch, etc), the battery widget can help you keep track of the battery life for each device.

Battery

Galaxy S23 Ultra		53%
S Pen		100%

Adding the widget is very simple:

- Tap and hold on the home screen, then select Widgets.
- Tap on the down arrow next to the Battery widget.
- You'll see two different styles: circles and list view; tap the one you want to display.
- The battery widget will now show all connected devices.
- You can go into your widget settings to change what displays and also adjust the color.

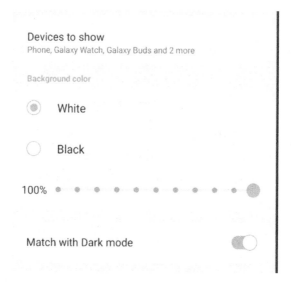

Devices to show
Phone, Galaxy Watch, Galaxy Buds and 2 more

Background color

⦿   White

◯   Black

100% • • • • • • • • • • ⬤

Match with Dark mode

WALLPAPER

Adding wallpaper to your screen is done in a similar way. Tap and hold your finger on the Home screen, when the menu comes up, select Wallpaper instead of Widgets.

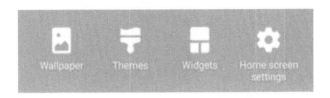

From the Wallpapers menu you have a few choices:

- My wallpapers – These are wallpapers you have purchased or ones that Samsung pre-loads.
- Gallery – Pictures you've taken.
- Explore more wallpapers – Where you can buy wallpapers.
- Color palette – this let's you choose a palette of colors based on the wallpaper that you select.

Wallpapers usually cost a buck. It's not an absurd amount of money, but you can also search for custom wallpapers on the Internet that are available for free.

Samsung's featured wallpapers should not be overlooked. There's a lot to choose from.

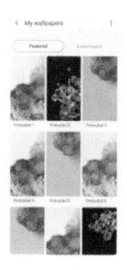

VIDEO WALLPAPER

One UI 5.1 added the ability to add video wallpaper; this only works on the lock screen–not your homescreen. You add video wallpaper the same way you do regular photos to your lock screen; the only difference is you pick a video instead.

THEMES

Picking wallpaper for your phone helps give it a bit more personality, but themes help really fine-tune the customization. You can pick icon shapes, fonts, and more.

To access them, press and hold on your Home screen, then select Themes.

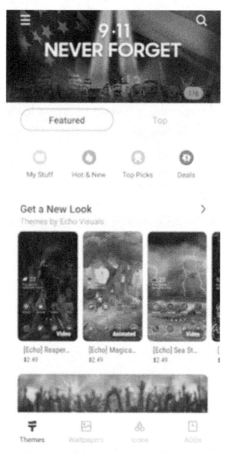

SAMSUNG FREE

Samsung Free is sort of like a recap of your day and daily recommendations for things to download. You can see it by swiping left from your Home screen.

It's not the worst feature on the phone, but a lot of people don't really see value in it. If you'd rather not see it, then tap and hold on your Home screen, then swipe left when you see the Home options. On the Samsung Daily preview, toggle the switch to off.

By default, you might have Google Discover turned on; Google Discover is the Google equivalent of Samsung Free.

ADDING SCREENS

Adding screens for even more shortcuts and widgets is easy. Tap and hold the Home screen, and swipe to the right.

Next, click the + icon which will add a screen. When you return to your Home screen, you can swipe right and start adding shortcuts and widgets to it.

HOME SCREEN SETTINGS

To access even more Home screen settings, tap and hold the Home screen, then tap the config Home screen settings icon.

The first area that you'll probably want to change is the Home screen layout.

< Home screen layout

A separate Apps screen will be available.
Swipe up or down on the Home screen to
show it.

◉ Home and Apps screens

○ Home screen only

Apply

The Home screen grid is also useful if you want to get a little more use out of the screen real estate; it adjusts icon size / placement to fit more or fewer icons on the screen.

The rest of the settings are just toggle switches.

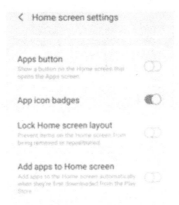

LOCK SCREEN

The lock screen is where you'll spend a lot of time; it helps you know if there's content worth unlocking your phone to see–new emails, messages, etc. But it can also start displaying too much content. If you find your lock screen is cluttered with information, then it's time to go into your settings and hide content.

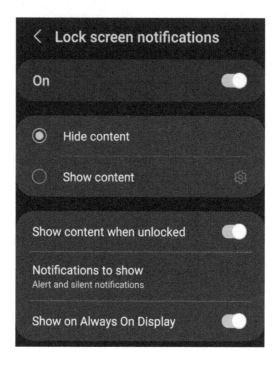

To use this feature, open your phone's settings and then go to Notifications; tap "Lock screen notification." You not will see all the options for how you want content displayed (or not displayed).

A WORD, OR TWO, ABOUT MENUS

It's pretty intuitive that if you tap on an icon, it opens the app. What's not so obvious is if you tap and hold there are other options. Every app is different. Usually, they're shortcuts—tapping and holding over the Phone icon, for example, brings up your favorites; doing the same thing over the camera brings up a selfie mode shortcut. Tap and hold over your favorite apps to see what shortcuts are available.

SPLIT SCREENS

The Samsung phone comes in different sizes; a bigger screen obviously gives you a lot more space, which makes split screen apps a pretty handy feature. It works on the smaller Samsung as well, though it doesn't feel as effective on the smaller screen.

To use this feature, swipe up to bring up multitasking; next, tap the icon above the window you want to turn into split screen (note: this feature is not supported on all apps); if split screen is available, you'll see a menu that has an option for split screen.

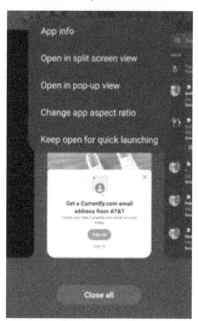

Once you tap split screen, it will let you swipe left and right to find the app you want to split the screen with. Tap the one you want.

Your screen is now split in two.

That thin blue bar in the middle is adjustable; you can move it up or down so one of the apps has more screen real estate.

To exit this mode, drag the black bar either all the way to the top or all the way to the bottom until one of the apps completely goes away.

MULTI-TASKING: POP-UP VIEW

Pop-Up View let's users drag a windows frame towards the edge of the screen to switch back to fullscreen mode.

GESTURES

Samsung has a few gestures built into the device that you can access by going into your settings app, then clicking Advanced features.

The first area to check out is Motions and gestures.

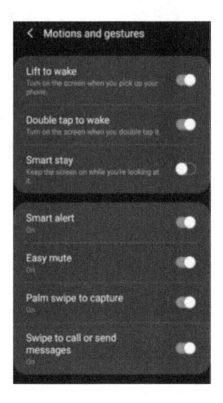

These are all toggle switches and you can see a preview of how they work by tapping on the title of the gesture.

The other setting is for One-handed mode. This is turned off by default. By toggling it on, you can see the options available to you.

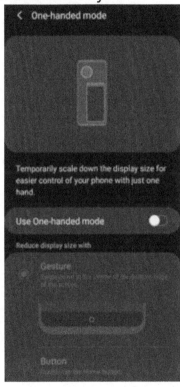

[4]

THE BASICS

Now that you have your phone set up and know your way around the device at its most basic level, let's go over the apps you'll be using the most that are currently on your shortcut or favorite bar:

- Phone
- Messages
- Chrome

Notice that Camera is off this list? There's a lot to cover with Camera, so I'll go over it in a separate chapter. In its place, I will cover the Google Play Store here, so you can begin downloading apps.

Before we get into it, there's something you need to know: how to open apps not on your favorite bar. It's easy. From your Home screen, swipe up from the middle of the screen. Notice that menu that's appearing? That's where all the additional apps are.

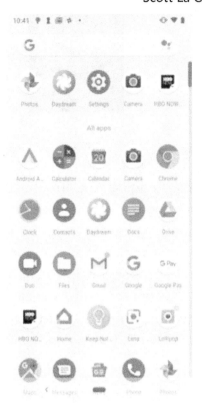

AI

AI (artificial intelligence) is huge on the Galaxy phone. I'll go over some of the many places you can use it (and how to turn it off), but as an intro just know that when you see the following icon, you can do something AI related (from translate text to manipulate an image.

MAKING CALLS

So...who you going to call? Ghostbusters?!

You would be the most awesome person in the world if Ghostbusters was in your phone contacts! But before you can find that number in your contacts, it would probably help to know how to add a contact, find a contact, edit a contact, and put contacts into groups, right? So before we get to making calls, let's do baby steps and cover Contacts.

CONTACTS

So, let's open up the Contacts app to get started. See it? Not on your favorite bar, right? So where is it?! That's why I showed you earlier how to get to additional apps. Swipe up from the middle of your Home screen and keep swiping until the menu appears in its entirety.

It's in alphabetical order, so the Contacts app is in the Cs. It looks like this:

Chances are if you've added your email account, you'll already have a lot of contacts listed. Like hundreds! There's going to be a message about merging them—that's up to you.

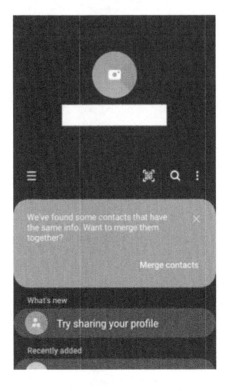

You can either search for the contact by clicking the magnifying glass, scroll slowly, or head to the right-hand side of the app and scroll—this lets you quickly scroll by letters. Just slide your finger until you see the letter of the contact you want and then stop.

I'm getting ahead of myself, however! Before you can scroll, it would be nice to know how to add a contact so there are people to scroll to. To add a contact, tap on that plus sign.

Before adding the contact, it will ask you where you want it saved—your Samsung account, the phone or Google. It's entirely up to you, but saving it to Google might save you some trouble if you switch to a different phone manufacturer in the future.

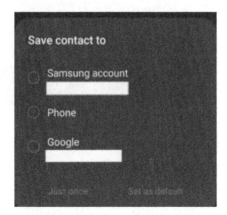

Adding a person looks more like applying for a job than adding a contact. There are rows and rows of fields!

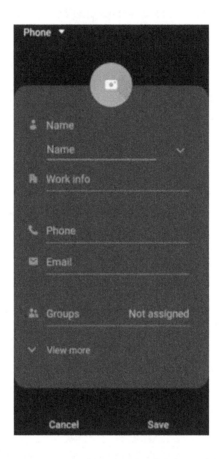

Just in case you weren't overwhelmed by all the fields, you can tap more fields and get even more!

Here's the most important thing you need to know: fields are optional! You can add a name and email and that's it. You don't even have to add their phone number. If you want to call them, then that would certainly help though.

If you have a hard time remembering who people are, then you can also take a picture or add a picture you already have. Comes in handy if you have eight kids and you can't remember if Joey is the one with blonde hair or red hair. Just tap the camera icon up top, then tap either Gallery (to assign a photo you've already taken) or Camera (to take a picture of them); you can also use one of the avatar type icons Samsung has.

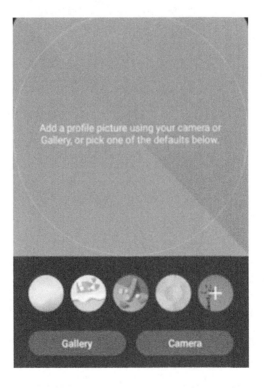

Once you are done, tap the save button.

EDITING A CONTACT

If you add an email and then later decide you should add a phone number, or if you want to edit anything else, then just find the name in your contacts and tap it once. This brings up all the info you've already added.

Go to the bottom of the screen and tap on the Edit option button. This makes the contact editable. Go to your desired field and update. When you are finished make sure to tap Save.

SHARING A CONTACT

If you have your phone long enough, someone will ask you for so-and-so's phone number. The old-fashioned way was to write it down. But you have a smartphone, so you aren't old-fashioned!

The new way to share a number is to find the person in your contacts, tap their name, then tap Share on the bottom left corner of the screen.

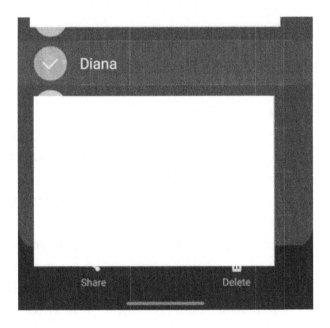

From here you have a few options, but the easiest is to text or email the contact to your friend. This sends them a contact card. So if you have other information with that contact (such as email) then that will be sent over as well.

DELETE CONTACT

Deleting a contact is the same as sharing a contact. The only difference is once you tap their name, you tap the delete icon to the right (not the share to the left). This erases them from your phone, but not your life.

GET ORGANIZED

Once you start getting lots of contacts, then it's going to make finding someone more time-consuming. Groups helps. You can add a Group for "Family" for instance, and then stick all of your family members there.

When you open your contacts and tap those three lines in the upper left corner, you'll see a menu. This is where you'll see your Groups. So with Groups, you can jump right into that list and find the contact you need.

You can also send the entire group inside the Group an email or text message. So for instance, if your child is turning two and you want to remind everyone in your "Family" contact not to come, then just tap on that Group.

But what if you don't have labels? Or if you want to add people to a label? Easy. Remember that long application you used to add a contact? One of the fields was called "Groups." You have to tap more to see it. It's all the way at the bottom. One of the last fields, in fact.

If you've never added a label or want to add a new one, then just start typing. If you have another one that you'd like to use, then just tap the arrow and select it.

When you are done, don't forget to tap Save.

You can also quickly assign someone to a group by tapping on the contact's name, then selecting Create Group from the upper right.

Once you tap that, you'll get to add a name, assign a ringtone, and assign other members.

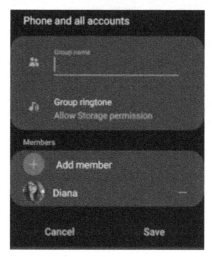

DELETE GROUP

If you decide you no longer want to have a la-bel, then just go to the menu I showed you above—side menu, then the three dots. From here, tap the Delete Group.

If there's just one person you want to boot from the label, then tap them and go to the Group and delete it.

MAKING CALLS

That concludes our sidetrack into the Contacts app. We can now get back to making phone calls to the Ghostbusters.

You can make a call by opening the Contacts app, then selecting the contact, and then tapping on their phone number. Alternatively, you can tap on the Phone button from your Home screen or favorite bar.

There are a few options when you open this app. Let's talk about each one.

Starting from the far left is the Keypad tab. It's green because you are already there.

In the middle is the Recents tab. If you've made any calls, they'll show here.

The last option is Contacts, which opens a version of the Contacts app that's within the Phone app.

If you want to dial someone the old-fashioned way by tapping in numbers, then tap them, and tap the call icon. You can also tap the video icon to start a video call.

When you are done with the call, hit the End button on your phone.

ANSWER AND DECLINE CALLS

What do you do when someone calls you? Probably ignore it because it's a telemarketer!

It's easy to accept a call, however. When the phone rings, the number will appear and if the person is in your Contacts, then the name will appear as well. To answer, just swipe the "answer." To decline just drag the "decline."

PHONE SETTINGS

If you haven't noticed already, there are settings for pretty much everything. Samsung is a *highly* customizable phone. To get to settings, go to the upper right corner, then select Settings.

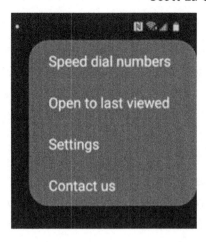

From settings you can set up ringtones, add numbers to block, set up your voicemail and much more.

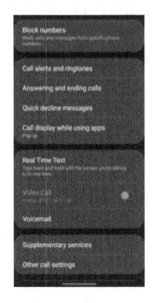

PLAY ANGRY BIRDS WHILE TALKING TO ANGRY MOM

What if you're on a call with your mom and she's just complaining about something, but you don't want to be rude and hang up? Easy. You multitask! This means you could play Angry Birds while talking!

To multitask, just swipe up from the bottom of your phone and open the app you want to work in while you are talking. The call will show in the notification area. Tap it to return to the call.

MESSAGES

Now that you know how Contacts and Phone works, messaging will be like second nature. They share many of the same properties.

Let's open up the Messages app (it's on your Favorites Bar).

CREATE / SEND A MESSAGE

When you have selected the contact(s) to send a message to, tap Compose. You can also manually type in the number in the text field.

You can add more than one contact—this is known as a group text.

The first time you send a message, it's going to probably look pretty bare like the image below. Assuming you have never sent one, it's going to be blank. Once you start getting messages, you can tap on New category to create labels for them—so all your family messages, for example, will be in one place.

Once you are ready to send your first message, tap the message icon.

The top field is where you put who it's going to (or the group name if it's several people). You can use the + icon to find people in your contacts.

Use the text field to type out your message.

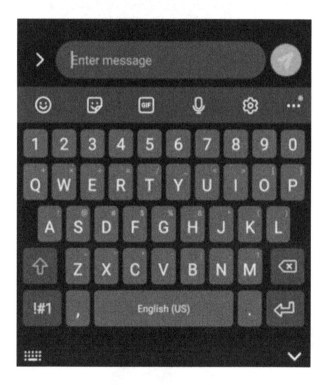

It looks pretty basic, but there's actually a *lot* here. Starting on the bottom, there's a little keyboard—that's to switch to a different type of keyboard; to the right of that is a down arrow, which will collapse the keyboard. To get it back, just click the message box again.

Just above the keyboard icon, is a !#1 button, which will switch the alpha keyboard to a numeric / symbol keyboard (so you have quick access to symbols like @, ?, %).

Typing in another language or need an accent sign? Long press the letter and you'll reveal more characters and symbols for that letter.

Finally, at the top is a set of six additional icons.

From left to right, the first is the Emoji pack. If you want to respond to someone with an Emoji, then that's what you tap.

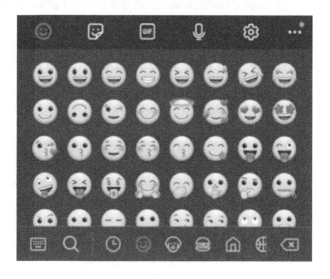

You can scroll through all of them by swiping right, but because there's so many of them, they are also grouped together, and you can jump to a group by tapping on the associated image on the bottom.

Next to the Emoji icon is the Bitmoji sticker icon. I'll cover Bitmoji later, but for now, let's just say Bitmoji is like an emoji that is customized to look like you. To use it, you have to download it. It's free.

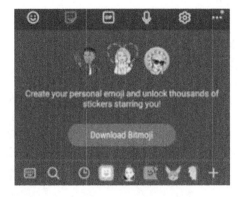

Next is the GIF search; you have to agree to the terms to use it. It's basically a search engine for GIF images; so if you want to find a birthday GIF to put in a message, for example, you could search "birthday" and see literally dozens and dozens of GIFs. If you don't know what a GIF is, they are small images that move on a loop—kind of like mini movies that last a couple seconds.

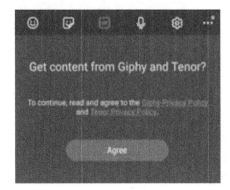

To the right of the GIF icon is the microphone icon, which lets you record a voice message instead of typing it.

You know Samsung loves its settings, so it probably won't surprise you that the config icon launches keyboard settings.

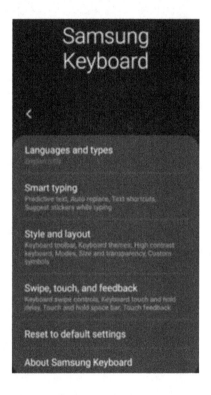

Because they love settings so much, there are a few more when you tap the three dots; you can adjust the keyboard size here, but also use some of the many other features—such as text editing and translation.

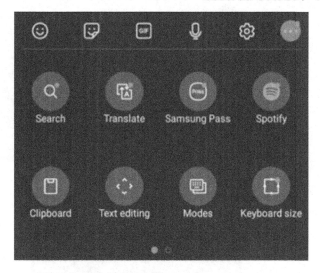

So, like I said, there's a lot to this keyboard. But the keyboard is only half the fun! Look above it...that little > icon will bring out some more things you can do with the message.

There are three additional options. The first is to include a picture that's in your photo gallery.

The next is to either take a photo or record a video.

And the last is a series of extra options.

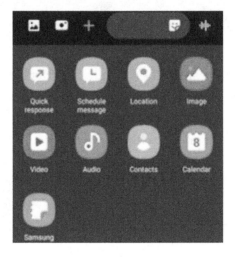

From left to right starting at the top:

- Quick response – Gives a list of common responses so you don't have to type anything.
- Schedule message – Lets you define when the message will be sent.
- Location – Shares where you are currently located with a person. So if a person is meeting you and they're saying

"I'm looking for you, but don't see you!" you can send this to give them a better idea.

- Image / Video – this is similar to adding a video / image from your gallery (you can actually do that here as well), but it also searches for them in other places like Google Drive.
- Audio – Share an audio file.
- Contacts – Share someone's contact information.
- Calendar – Share an event in your calendar with another person.
- Samsung – Share a Samsung Note with a person.

When you are ready to send your message, tap the arrow with the SMS under it.

VIEW MESSAGE

When you get a message, your phone will vibrate, chirp, or do nothing—it all depends on how you set up your phone. To view the message, you can either open the app, or swipe down to see your notifications—one will be the text message.

WHERE'S AN APP FOR THAT?

I mentioned earlier that you could play Angry Birds while talking to your angry mom on the phone. Sound fun? But where is Angry Birds on your phone? It's not! You have to download it.

Adding and removing apps on the Galaxy is easy. Head to your favorite bar on the bottom of your Home screen and tap the Google Play app.

This launches the Play Store.

From here you can browse the top apps, see editors' picks, look through categories, or, if you have an app in mind, search for it. The Play Store isn't just for apps. You can use the tabs on the top to go to movies, books, and music. Any kind of downloadable content that's offered by Google can be found here.

When you see the app you want, tap on it. You can read through reviews, see screenshots, and install it on your phone. To install, simply tap the install button—if it's a paid app you'll be prompted to buy it. If there's no price, it's free (or offers in-app payments—which means the app is free, but there are premium features inside it you may have to pay for).

The app is now stored in the app section of your device (remember the section you get to when you swipe up from the bottom to the top?).

REMOVE APP

If you decide you no longer want an app, go to the app in the app menu and tap and hold it. This brings up a box with a few options. The one you want is Uninstall.

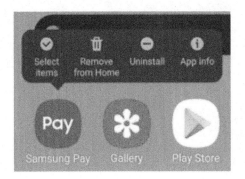

If you downloaded the app from the Play Store, you can always delete it. Some apps that were pre-installed on your phone cannot be deleted.

DRIVING DIRECTIONS

Back in the day, you may have had a GPS. It was a fancy plastic device that would give you directions for anywhere in North America. You can throw out that device because your phone is your new GPS.

To get directions, swipe up to open up your apps, and go to the Google folder. Tap the Maps app.

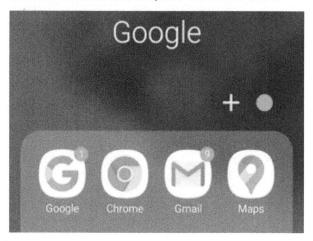

It's automatically going to be set to wherever you are currently at—which is both creepy and useful.

To get started, just type where you want to go. I'm searching for Disneyland, Anaheim.

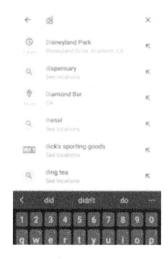

It automatically starts filling in what it thinks you are going to type and tells you the distance. When you see the one you want, tap it.

It pinpoints the location on the map and also gives you an option to call, share or get directions to the location. If you want to zoom out or in, just use two fingers and pinch in or out on the screen.

It automatically gets directions from where you are. Want it from a different location? Just tap on the "Your location" field and type where you want to go. You can also reverse the directions by tapping on the double arrows. When you are ready to go, tap Start.

What if you don't want to drive? What if you want to walk? Or bike? Or take a taxi? There are options for all of those and more! Tap the slider under the address bar to whatever you prefer. This updates the directions—when you walk, for example, it will show you one-way streets and also update the time it will take you.

What if you want to drive but are like me: terrified of freeways in California? There's an option to avoid highways. Tap the menu button in the upper right corner of the screen and select Route options (there are actually lots of other things packed in here like adding stops, sharing directions, and sharing your location).

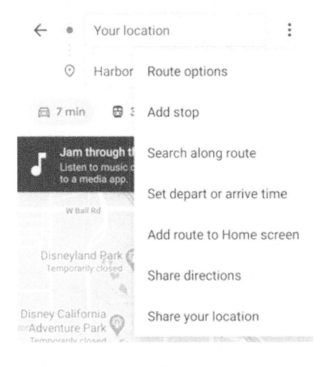

In the Route options, select what you want to avoid, and hit Done. You are now rerouted to a longer route—notice how the times probably changed?

Once you get your directions, you can swipe up to get turn-by-turn directions.

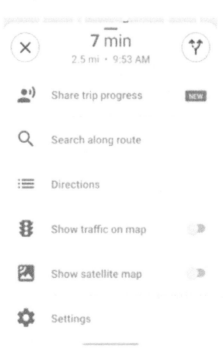

You can even see what it looks like from the street. It's called Street View.

Street View isn't only for streets. Google is expanding the feature everywhere. If you hold your finger over the map, there will be an option to show Street View if it's available. Just tap the thumbnail. Here's a Street View of Disneyland:

You can wander around the entire park! If only you could ride the rides, too! You can get even closer to the action by picking up the Dreamview headset. When you stick your phone in that, you can turn your head and the view turns with you.

Street View is also available in a lot of malls and other tourist attractions. Point your map to the Smithsonian in Washington, DC and get a pretty cool Street View.

LIVE CAPTIONING

One of the bigger features to Android 10 is live captioning; live captioning can transcribe any video you record and show what's being said. It works surprisingly well and is pretty accurate.

To turn it on, go to Settings > Accessibility > Hearing enhancements > Live caption.

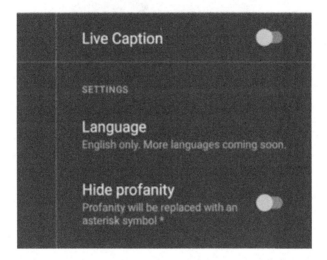

In the settings, you can also toggle off profanity, and, coming soon, select a different language. If it's something you'd only occasionally use, I recommend leaving it toggled off, but having it toggled on under Live Caption in volume control. With that toggled on, all you have to do is press the volume button. Once you do that, you'll see the option to turn it on; it's the bottom option.

Once it's on, you'll start seeing a transcription appear in seconds.

REFRESH RATE

The Galaxy supports up to 120Hz refresh rate. Wow, right? Actually, most people have no idea what this means. It's frames per second (FPS)—or 120 FPS. So, what does that mean? If you're playing games or using something that has fast moving action, it means things will seem a lot smoother. It will also eat your battery life to shreds, so use with caution (60Hz is the norm). The battery life for 120 FPS is much better on newer Galaxy phones.

To toggle it on go to Settings > Display > Motion smoothness.

Next, select 120 Hz.

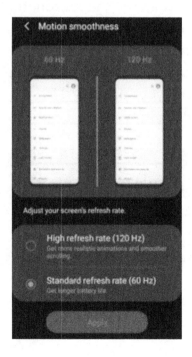

I recommend turning it on just to see what it looks like, but if you are not just absolutely blown away by it, then turn it off so you can have a longer lasting battery.

SHARING WI-FI

Anytime you have guests over, you almost always get the question: what's your wi-fi password? If you are like me, then it probably annoys you. Maybe your password is really long, maybe you just don't like giving out your password, or maybe you are just too embarrassed to say that it's "Feet$FetishLover1." Whatever the reason, then you will love sharing your wi-fi with QR codes. Gone are the days of giving this info out. Just give them a code that they scan, and they'll have access without ever knowing what your password is.

To use it, go to your wi-fi settings, then select the Wi-Fi options and Wi-Fi Direct.

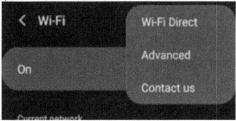

Make sure both devices have Wi-Fi on and follow the directions.

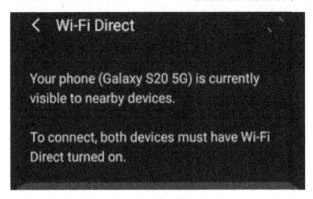

CIRCLE TO SEARCH

Samsung has partnered with Google to showcase the power of AI on the phone. One that you might find yourself using a lot of is Circle to Search.

Circle to Search is not anything groundbreaking—Google has been doing reverse image searching for years and has offered Google Lenes for a long time. What makes Circle to Search so nice is how easy it is to use.

So, what is it exactly? Imagine you're reading a news story and there's a photo of someone, but you don't know who. You can circle it to see who! You can circle objects, text—anything!

How does it work? Press and hold the home button.

Your screen will change shades to indicate that it's active. Now circle whatever you want to find information on.

That's it! In seconds your see information about whatever you just selected.

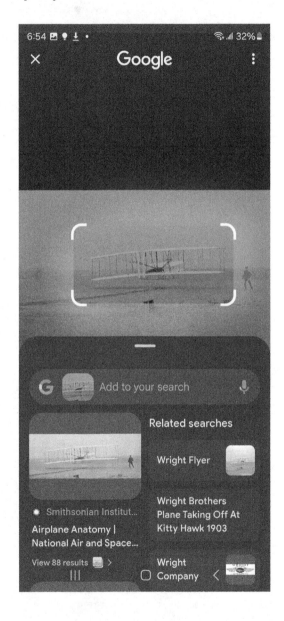

SUMMARIZE

When you are using Samsung's web browser, you can use AI to summarize whatever you are reading. Just tap the AI button in the middle bottom of your screen.

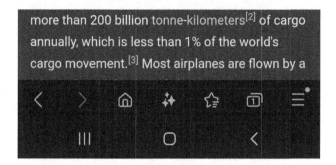

This will ask you if you want to summarize or translate what you are reading.

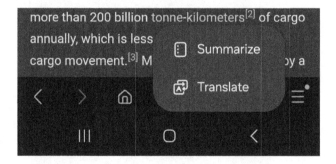

In just a few seconds, you'll have a bullet point summary of the article you are reading!

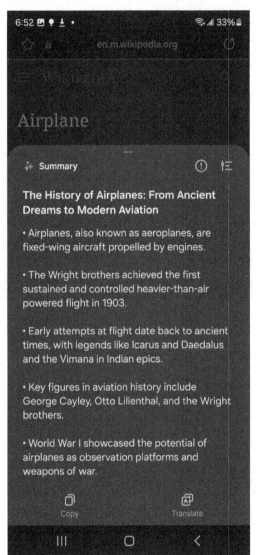

KIDS HOME

One place Samsung truly shines above other companies is with its parental control features and kids mode. Yes, other devices have parental controls, but Samsung takes it up a notch by creating a UI that's just for kids.

With kids mode, you can quickly toggle it on and off for those moments where you need to distract a child.

To access it, swipe down to bring down your notification bar, then swipe right one time. It's one of the notifications icons that you'll need to manually add to use.

The first time you launch it, you'll have to download a very small program. It will take a few seconds depending on your connection speed.

Once it's done downloading, you'll see the welcome screen and be asked if you want to create a shortcut on your desktop. Tap Start when you are ready.

Once you tap Next, you'll get to the main Samsung Kids UI. It looks a little like your phone...only cuter! There's a handful of icons on the screen, but you'll notice they each have download buttons. That's because they aren't installed yet. You have to tap the download button for each app you want to install (not more than three at a time).

Swipe to your left, and you'll see non-Samsung apps. These need to be downloaded as well.

You might be thinking, how safe can this mode be? There's an Internet browser right on the Home screen! Tap it and let's see!

You'll notice right away that this is not yo mama's Internet! The only websites they can access are the ones you add. Want to add one? Tap the +New website button.

You'll quickly notice that all the apps in this mode are very stripped down. Even the camera app, which is pretty harmless, has few features. There's a shutter, a toggle for photos and videos, and a button for effects.

The phone is the same way. Your child can't open the app and call anyone. They can only call numbers that you've added. Want to add someone? Just tap the + icon.

The pre-installed apps are all pretty harmless, and borderline educational.

If there's apps you want to remove or install, then tap the option button in the upper right corner.

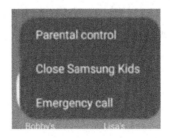

Once you put in your pin, you'll have access to the settings. Here you'll be able to control what your child does and how long they do it for. You can also monitor what they've been doing. You can control how much time they can spend on something like games and something like reading.

Is there a pre-installed app that you don't want your child to see? No problem! Scroll down a little and tap the Apps option.

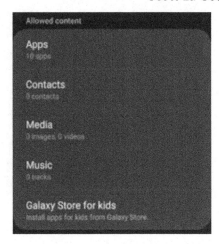

From the options button, select Remove and then select the app that you want removed.

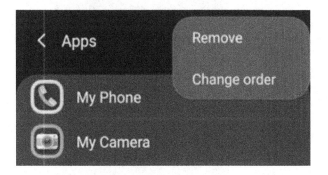

What about other apps? Like third-party ones? Return to that list and select Galaxy Store for kids. That's going to take you to a custom kids' store. It's not going to have teen or adult games—it's only games that are appropriate for kids.

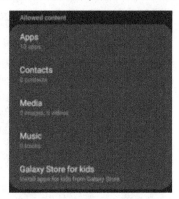

Tap the download option next to any app that you want to download. They'll show up when you swipe right from kids Home screen.

So that's all well and good, but what happens when you want to return to adulthood? How do you get out of this mode? It takes just a second! On the Home screen, tap the back icon. It will ask you for your pin code. Once you add it, you are back in normal mode. That's it!

SMARTTAGS

If you bought your Galaxy phone when it was first released, then chances are it was bundled with a SmartTag; if not, it is $29.99.

SmartTag is an optional accessory for finding your gadgets and devices. You can attach it to your king ring, stick it on a remote, put it in your purse, or wherever you might lose something. If you can't find your keys, then from your phone you can ping it and the SmartTag will start ringing.

You can also connect your SmartTag to smart home devices like lights and doors; so when you come up, you can double click your tag to perform an action—like turn on the lights.

SmartTag connects to your phone with Bluetooth and runs on a battery. As long as you aren't pinging your device every five minutes, you shouldn't have to replace the battery very often.

To get started, go to the SmartThings app from the Samsung folder of all apps; if you don't have it, you can download it free from the app store. It's included with the newest OS update, so chances are it's there if you have a new phone.

The first time the app opens, you'll have to agree to the terms and conditions.

Welcome to
SmartThings

Take a look at the policies below

○ Privacy Policy

○ I agree to all.

SmartThings also needs the following permissions

📍   Location
Used to scan for nearby devices using Bluetooth Low Energy (BLE), to locate your devices, and to create automations based on your location

SmartThings automatically turns on Wi-Fi and Bluetooth to scan for devices. You can change this in Settings.

Once you click start, press the button on the tag and it should find it right away. Make sure and tap "While using the app" on the next screen.

If the tag will always be in a particular room, then you can name it; otherwise just skip it.

Next it will ask if you want to add the device now or later. Tap Add Now.

Next, confirm that the tag can know your location. It needs to know the location to properly work.

Click start next.

It will take a few seconds to set everything up.

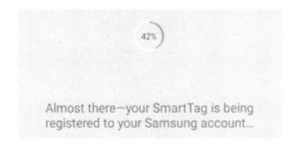

When it's done, you'll be prompted to name the tag. You can keep it as SmartTag, but being more descriptive (i.e. calling it car keys) is advisable if you have several SmartTag's.

You'll see a couple of setup screens, then it will ask you if you want to update the SmartTag; I recommend doing this. It is very quick and it makes sure the SmartTag is free of any bugs.

Once it's done, you'll see your main screen; click Get Started.

Next, download the add-on software.

To use all the features of SmartThings Find, an add-on needs to be downloaded.

Cancel   Download

Once you're finished, you can open the software again and you'll be able to tap the music icon to ping your SmartTag; when you do, it will start to ring.

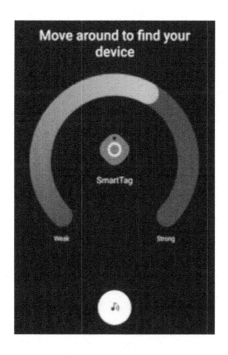

[5]

INTERNET

When it comes to the Internet, there are two things you'll want to do:
- Send email
- Browse the Internet

ADD AN EMAIL ACCOUNT

When you set up your phone, you'll set it up to your Google Account, which is usually your email.

You may, however, want to add another email account—or remove the one you set up.

To add an email, swipe up to bring up your apps, and tap on Settings.

Next, tap on Accounts.

From here, select Add Account; you can also tap on the account that's been set up and tap remove account—but remember you can have more than one account on your phone.

Once you add your email, you'll be asked what type of email it is. Follow the steps after you select the email type to add in your email, password, and other required fields.

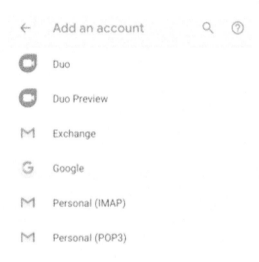

CREATE AND SEND AN EMAIL

To send an email using Gmail (Samsung's native email app), swipe up to get to your apps, tap Gmail, and tap Compose a New Email (the little round, red pencil in the lower right corner). When you're done, tap the Send button.

You can also use the Google Play Store to find other email apps (such as Outlook).

MANAGE MULTIPLE EMAIL ACCOUNTS

If you have more than one Gmail account, tap the three lines at the upper left of your email screen; this brings out a slider menu. If you tap on the little arrow next to the email address, it drops down and will show other accounts. If none are listed, you can add one.

SURFING THE INTERNET

Google's native Web browser is Chrome. You can use other browsers (which can be found in the Google Play Store). This book will only cover Chrome, however.

Get started by tapping on the Chrome browser icon from your favorite bar, or by going into all programs.

If you've used Chrome on a desktop or any other device, then this chapter won't exactly be rocket science—just like the email app, many of the same properties you find on the desktop exist on the mobile version.

When you open it, you'll see it's a pretty basic browser. There are three main things that you'll want to note.

- **Address Bar** - As you would guess, this is where you put the Internet address you want to go to (google.com, for example); what you should understand, however is that this is not just an address bar. This is a search bar. You can use it to search for things just as you would searching for something on Google; when you hit the enter key, it takes you to the Google search results page.

- **Tab Button** - Because you are limited in space, you don't actually see all your tabs like you would on a normal browser; instead you get a button that tells you how many tabs are open. If you tap it, you can either toggle between the tabs, or swipe over one of the pages to close the tab.

- **Menu Button** - The last button brings up a menu with a series of other options that I'll talk about next.

The menu is pretty straightforward, but there are a few things worth noting.

"New incognito tab" opens your phone into private browsing; that doesn't mean your IP isn't tracked. It means your history isn't record; it also means passwords and cookies aren't stored.

A little bit further down is "History"; if you want your history erased so there's no record on your phone of where you went, then go here and clear your browsing history.

If you want to erase more than just websites (passwords, for example) then go to Settings at the very bottom of the menu. This opens up more advanced settings.

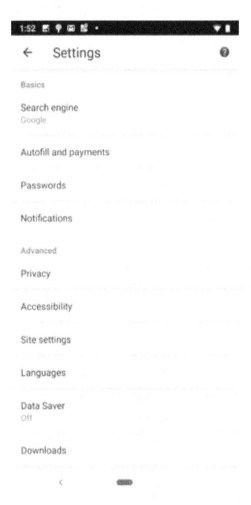

[6]

SNAP IT!

The camera is the bread and butter of the Samsung phone. Many people consider the Samsung Galaxy to be the greatest camera ever on a phone. I'll leave that for you to decide. Personally, I think all top tier phone cameras have their own pros and cons.

This chapter is based off the Galaxy Ultra. As mentioned earlier in the book, not all smartphones are alike in terms of cameras; it's one of the most noticeable differences with the phones. The Ultra has more lens, more zoom and more pixels.

This means that if you are using a non-Ultra phone, some of the things mentioned in this chapter won't apply to you. So if you are reading and thinking "where is that on my phone" then you probably don't have an Ultra.

THE BASICS

Are you ready to get your Ansel Adams on? Let's get started by opening the Camera app

When you open the app, it starts in the basic camera mode. The UI can look pretty simple, but don't be fooled. There are a lot of controls.

On the bottom of the screen is the shutter (to take your photo)—swipe it down to take a "burst shot" which takes several photos at once, and hold it down to toggle to video. To the right of the shutter is the camera flip—to switch to the front camera.

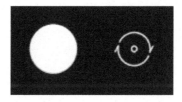

Up on the top of the camera app is where you'll find the majority of your settings.

Starting from left to right, there is the settings icon. Most of the settings are just toggle switches and easy to understand.

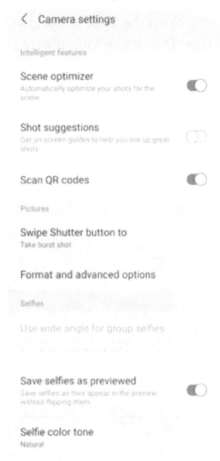

Next to that is the flash setting. Tapping that will let you select no flash, auto flash, or force flash.

The next option is the timer. This lets you delay when the photo will be taken. It's best used with a tripod.

The next option lets you pick how large the photo will be. The best option is 108 MB. That's going to give you an unbelievably *huge* image. It's also going to take away the next two options. If you notice they're grayed out…that's why. This is the only mode that you cannot use them on.

And what are those two options? The first toggles Motion on and off. And the second lets you use special filters to enhance the photo.

One final note on photos (and this applies to videos as well): to zoom, you pinch in and out.

CAMERA MODES

Taking pictures is so yesterday though, isn't it? Smartphones are loaded with different modes and Samsung is obviously no stranger to some really great ones.

Think of modes like different lenses. You have your basic camera lens, but then you can also have a lens for fisheye and close up. If you look at the bottom of your camera app, you can slide left and right to get to the different modes.

There are three main ones in the app: photos (which I covered above), videos, and Single Take.

If you've had a smartphone before, then video will probably be familiar to you, but Single Take will probably be new.

Quickly, the video mode has similar features to photo mode. Starting at the bottom, you can pick the kind of video you are taking—three leaves will pull the zoom back and give a wider shot, and one leaf will pull it in and give a closer one.

Up on top, the menu is largely the same as the photo one.

I'll point out one thing, however: the 9:16 icon will launch the video ratio. Video can actually record all the way to 8K! But be careful! As you probably can guess, an 8K video is going to be *huge*. One advantage to that mode is you are able to pull pretty good still photos from the video.

Just like the other modes, pinching in and out will let you zoom in and out.

Single Take is a pretty cool mode. When you press it, it starts recording a 15 second clip. There are no filters or ratios you can change here. It's stripped down.

The beauty of this mode is what it's doing is using a computer to pick the best photo from the video. When the fifteen seconds are up, it will start populating them.

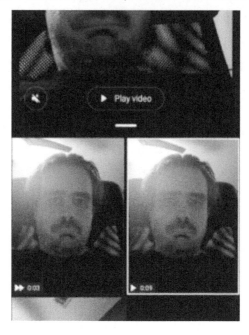

If you click the More option on the slider, you'll see that there are actually several more photography modes on the phone. Twelve more modes to be exact.

AR Doodle used to be a feature in video recording, but it's now been moved to its own camera mode. The mode let's draw things as you record.

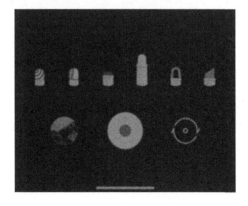

If you thought the Photo mode was a little lacking in options and settings, wait until you see the Pro mode!

You can adjust things like ISO, auto focus and more.

There's also a Pro Video mode with a similar feature set.

Panorama lets you create a panoramic photo; it's great for landscape and cityscape shots.

Food changes settings to give the most ideal focus and effects to take food photos.

Night mode will help you get great shots in low lighting.

Portrait and Portrait Video (previously called Live Focus and Live Focus Video) are great for close up shots of people where you want to blur the background.

Super Slow-Mo, Slow motion and Hyperlapse let you capture either slow motion videos or time-lapse videos.

The final mode is called Director's View, and it's pretty awesome! It lets you record video with both the front and back facing camera at the same time. It's perfect for capturing people's reaction, doing tours, and more. When you use it, you'll see the main screen, then the other camera in the lower left corner.

Tap the arrow above Director's View to toggle between the camera you are using. Just tap the preview to switch.

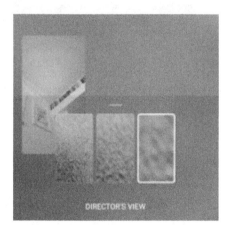

EXPERT RAW

You might be familiar with RAW; but Expert RAW? What's that all about? Shooting in RAW is something only on the Ultra Samsung devices; it's a professional camera setting that uses much more data than a traditional JPEG photo–to be clear: this is something you want to be careful with because it's going to take up much more space and be harder to share.

By default the camera will shoot with a traditional JPEG or HEIC file format. When it does this, it's creating a single file format. It's perfect for most people. But photographers like to edit photos, and that's where Expert RAW comes in. Expert RAW creates a multi-frame, which gives much more flexibility for editing a photo.

Expert Raw used to be an app you downloaded from the app store; but with One UI 5.1, it is now integrated into the camera app–while still an app in itself. To use it (if your phone supports it), go to the More tab in the camera app; the setting is a shortcut and will take you to the Expert Raw app–a download may be needed.

COLOR TONE ON SELFIE

The Selfie camera features two color tones: Natural and Bright. By default, Natural Tone is selected. As the name implies, bright will brighten up your normal tone.

To use it turn on the selfie camera, then tap the effects button in the top right corner (looks a little like a wand). From here, select the Color Tone option, then toggle between Natural or Bright.

EDITING PHOTOS

Once you take a photo, you can begin fine-tuning it to really make it sparkle. You can access editing by opening the photo you want to make edits to. This is done by either opening it from the camera app by clicking on the photo preview (next to the shutter):

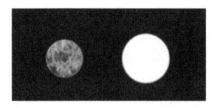

Or by opening the Photo app.

Later in this chapter, I'll write a bit more about how photos are organized, and how you can change things around. For now, we are just talking about editing a photo, so for the purpose of this section, tap on any photo to edit it.

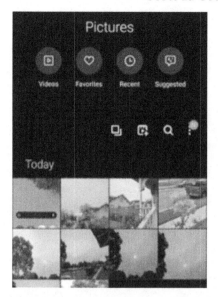

When you open a photo, the options you see will vary depending on what kind of photo you open.

The below example is a Live Focus photo.

As the name suggests, the background is blurred. There's also an option here: Change background effect. This technically isn't editing a photo—when you edit a photo, you go into a different app.

When you tap change the background, you'll have four options. With each option, you can change the intensity of the blur with the slider.

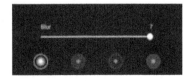

The main blur is simply called "blur"; the next is a spin blur.

The third is a zoom blur.

The last type of blur is color point, which makes the object color and the background black and white.

If you make any changes here, always make sure and tap Apply to save it.

Single Take photos also work a little differently when it comes to editing because you have to select which photo you want to edit.

Regardless of the type of photo, there are going to be several options that are the same. Starting on the top, that little play icon will wirelessly show your photo on another device (like a compatible TV).

Next to the play icon is an icon that looks kind of like an eye. That will digitally scan your photo and try and identify what the photo is. In the below example, it finds a flower and gives a link to see more. This feature works pretty well, but isn't always perfect.

Next to the eye icon is an option icon. This will let you set a photo as wallpaper, print it, etc. If you tap Details, it will also let you see when the photo was taken, its resolution, and any tags that have been assigned to it.

On the bottom of any photo are four additional options. The heart icon favorites the photo, the pencil lets you edit it (more on that in a second), the three dots lets you share it, and the trash lets you delete it.

Tap the pencil icon and let's see how to edit a photo next. Regardless of the photo, you'll see the same options on the bottom.

The first option is to crop the photo. To crop, drag the little white corners.

Next is the filter option. The slider lets you select the type of filter, and below that is a slider to adjust the intensity of the filter.

Brightness is the next icon. Each icon here adjusts a different setting (such as the contrast of the photo).

The sticker icon will launch Bitmoji (I'll discuss this later in the chapter), but what this does is let you put stickers on top of your photo.

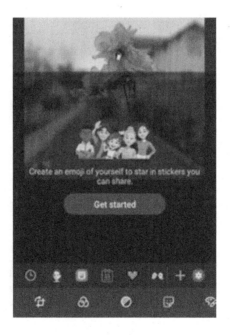

The paintbrush icon lets you draw on top of your photo.

And the text icon lets you write on top of your photo.

If you don't want to spend time editing your photo—you just want it to magically look better with no effort, there's an option up in the upper left corner that will do that for you—it crops, rotates, and adds a filter to it. Depending on how well you took the shot, you may not see much difference.

In the upper right corner is an options menu with even more choices for editing your picture.

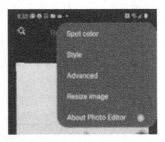

The first is Spot color. Using the little pickers, you can remove a color from the photo to make the subject stand out. To save any changes here, make sure and tap the checkmark; to cancel changes, tap the X.

Style applies filters that give the photo more of an artistic pop—if you want your photo to look like a painting, for example. The slider below it will adjust the intensity.

The advanced option will let you do color corrections.

If you took a photo at the highest resolution and are having difficulty sharing it, you can use the Resize image option to make it smaller.

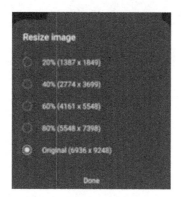

Once you are finished doing edits, make sure and tap Save.

EDITING VIDEOS

Editing a video shares a lot of common features to photos, so make sure and read that section first, as I will not repeat features already referenced above.

To get started open the video that you want to edit, then tap to play it. In the play window, there are going to be a couple of things you should note.

Over on the upper left side you'll see the icon below. This lets you capture a photo from the video. You can do it with any resolution, but you'll find the best photos will come from an 8K video.

Over on the upper right side is a GIF button. This will let you create a GIF from your video.

You'll notice the video has the same options at the bottom of it (assuming you haven't played it). To edit it, just tap on that pencil.

The first option you'll see is to crop the video. To crop just drag in or out the white bars before and after the video clip.

Next is the color filter, which works almost identically to the photo filter.

The text icon comes after this and lets you write on top of the photo.

The emoji sticker insert is after this.

And the paintbrush is second to last.

The last icon is for adding sound. You can add music or anything else you want. You can also use the slider under Video sound to make the videos original sound softer (or nonexistent)—so, for example, you could remove all sound from a family dinner, and replace it with music.

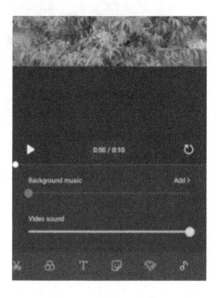

Up on top, there's one option: resolution. If you've recorded in 8K and it's too large, you can use this option to make it smaller.

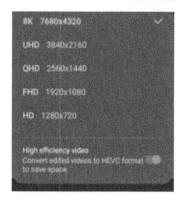

CUT OUT SUBJECT FROM PHOTO

If you long-press over the subject of a photo and wait, the object will be cutout of the photo and you can paste it anywhere else—such as a Google Doc or email; when it's pasted, only the subject will appear—the background will be removed.

ORGANIZING YOUR PHOTOS AND VIDEOS

The great thing about mobile photos is you always have a camera ready to capture memorable events; the bad thing about mobile photos is you always have a camera ready to capture events, and you'll find you have hundreds and hundreds of photos very quickly.

Fortunately, Samsung makes it very simple to organize your photos so you can find what you are looking for.

Let's open up the Gallery app and see how to get things organized.

Galaxy keeps things pretty simple by having only four options on the bottom of your screen.

There are four additional options up on top.

In the upper right corner, there's three dots, which is the photo option menu; that menu is there no matter where you are in the Gallery app.

When you tap that menu, you'll get several more options. From this menu you can share an album, create a GIF / collage / Slideshow of the album, or edit the photos / videos in it.

If there's something you are trying to find, tap on the magnifying glass. You can search by what it is (a Live Focus, video, etc.), you can search for tags, you can type an expression (happy photos, for example).

When you tap on Albums, you'll see your albums (Samsung will automatically create some for you), and you can tap on options to create a new album.

Stories lets you capture all your life adventures; you can create a new Story the same way you created an album.

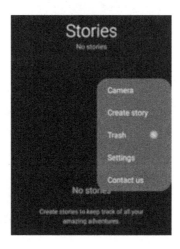

The last option is sharing your photos. To get started, tap the red button

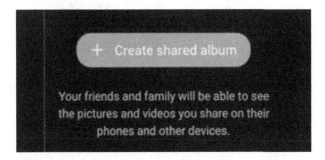

Next, type in a person's phone number or Samsung ID.

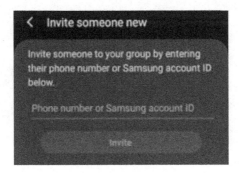

Once you have your shared album created, you can tap the + icon to add photos to it.

You don't have to add all the photos at once. You can continue to add them over time.

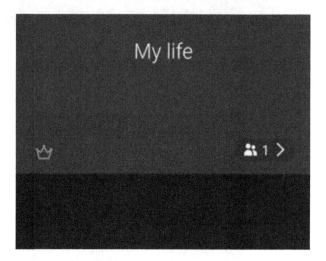

GALLERY SEARCH

Searching for photos is different than what you might be used to–or rather smarter than what you are used to. You can search for specific locations and people, but you can also search for items–so if the person was wearing sunglasses or a jacket.

BITMOJI

Bitmoji is the Samsung equivalent of Memoji on the iPhone; it basically lets you create an avatar of yourself that you can use in photos and text messages.

To get started, go to the Camera app, then select More, and finally tap AR Zone.

Next, tap the AR Emoji Camera option.

Before you can have fun, you'll need to take a picture of yourself. Make sure you are in an area with good lighting for the best results.

Once you take the photo, select the gender icon. They are as follows: adult male, adult female, male child, female child. Once you make your selecttion, you'll need wait a few seconds for it to analyze the photo.

Next, you can start using the options to change the way you look and what your avatar is wearing.

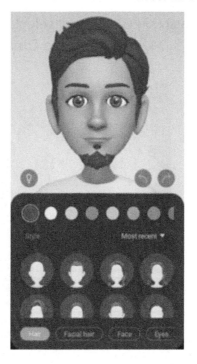

You will now be able to use your AR Camera to take photos with your avatar's head replacing other people's heads!

You can also slide over and select other pre-made avatars. My favorite is the Disney one.

On the bottom of the camera is a slider to select the different AR Camera modes. Mirror, for example, will put your avatar in the frame of the photo.

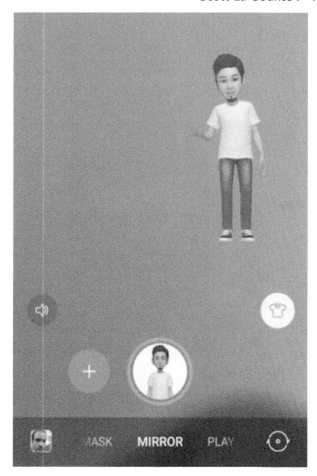

AI IMAGE IMPROVEMENTS

You already know that AI is big on the Galaxy, but I'm about to show you why it's not just "that's cool", rather it's "that's insane!" Because using it with images is incredible.

REMOVING PEOPLE

Look at the photo below of my child. Great! She's beautiful. But she's the center of my universe—I don't want those two kids sharing the frame!

To get these two kids out of the frame, I'm going to tap the AI button to switch from basic editing to AI editing.

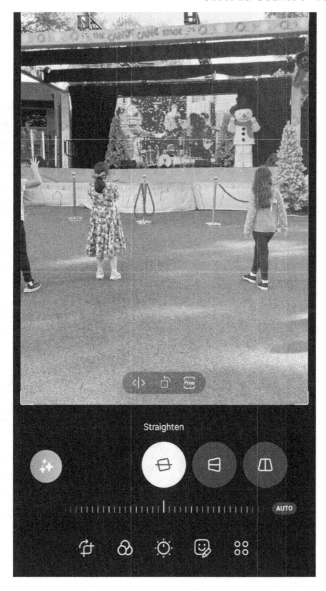

Next, I'm going to circle all the objects I want to remove. And you'll notice you don't have to be accurate—the AI will find the outlines you want; in the image below, you can see how the person on the right was already circled and now there's dotted lines tightly around only the person's body; the person on the left, I just circled, so it's a wide circle.

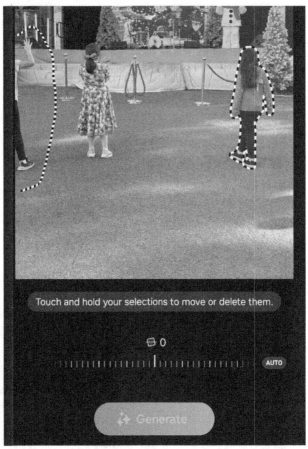

When I'm happy with everything, I'll tap and hold over a selected object. This will give me the option to undo it or erase it (we'll go over moving t next). When I'm happy with everything selected, I'll tap the Generate button.

It will take a few seconds to generate depending on its complexity. When you're done, the new photo will magically appear. Tapping on the "View Original" will toggle between the two images, so you can compare; tapping done will save the new AI generated image.

MOVING AN OBJECT OR PERSON

I mentioned earlier that you could move a person in addition to erasing them. It's just as easy as erasing them. You'll recall when you tap and hold over a selected object, the erase icon comes up? Well, you can also tap and drag it at this point.

In the image below, I've dragged the image and now there's checked squares where the image used to be (don't worry—that's going to be filled in).

But we are still not pushing the boundaries of what the AI editor can do. Using the four dots that outline the person or object, you can drag in or out to make them larger or smaller, or also rotate them. In the example below, I've made my daughter a little larger, then I also pulled out the snowman, brought him forward and made him larger.

The finished result is below; it's not always perfect, so you have to experiment. You can see in the below one that my daughter moved pretty well, but the snowman's hat looks a little off—probably because the hat was a black object against a black background, and it had difficulty picking up what was what. At quick glance, it's probably going to fool anyone who looks though.

STRAIGHTENING A PICTURE

If you've ever tried to straighten a picture, you've probably been annoyed that in doing so, it crops things you don't want cropped. AI solves this!

In AI mode, you'll notice a slider bar on the bottom to straighten object—dragging it left or right will make your photo look similar to what's below.

Here's how the feature shines; once you tap generate, it will start filling all those checked areas with an AI generated fill. You can see the result of this picture below.

ADDING AN OBJECT OR PERSON INTO PHOTO

Editing with AI is fun, but now I'm going to really push it by adding people into a scene.

I'm going to start with this landscape scene.

Next, I'm going to remove some buildings using the method used earlier.

Near the top of the photo, you'll probably have noticed the plus icon; that's what we want to tap next (if you don't see it, then you're probably not in AI editing). You can copy it from your clipboard or add it from your Gallery; I'm going to find another photo in my Gallery, so I'll select that one.

Once the gallery photo is open, you can tap and hold the object you want to move into the photo, and then tap Done in the bottom right corner.

Next move the object whenever you want (and remember you can rotate and make it bigger by dragging over the dots). You'll also notice the + icon is still there—that's because you can add multiple images. Once you're happy with every-thing, tap the generate button.

You now have a new photo with the object included in it. Pretty cool, huh?!

AI WATERMARK

Once you're done saving all your changes, you'll notice an AI watermark in the corner. This tells anyone looking that you used AI to generate the image. If you really hate that, you can use the remove tool to get rid of it.

USING NON-SAMSUNG PHOTOS

If your new to Samsung, then you probably have a lot of non-Samsung photos floating around other devices. The cool thing about these new AI tools is you can edit those photos as well! All you have to do is download them onto your phone. Once they're in your gallery, then you can edit away!

Personally, I use Google Photos to backup all my photos. So any device I have that takes photos also has the Google Photos app; they all backup to the cloud, so whenever I get a new device, they're all there. To get a photo onto my device, I open it there, and then select Save to Device.

[7]
GOING BEYOND

If you want to take total control of your Samsung, then you need to know where the system settings are and what can and can't be changed there.

First, the easy part: the system settings are located with the rest of your apps. Swipe up and scroll down to "Settings."

This opens all the settings available:
- Connections
- Sounds and vibrations

- Notifications
- Display
- Wallpaper
- Themes
- Home screen
- Lock screen
- Biometrics and security
- Privacy
- Location
- Accounts and backup
- Google
- Advanced features
- Digital Wellbeing and parental controls
- General Management
- Apps
- Battery and Device Management
- Accessibility
- Software update
- Tips and help
- About phone

I'll cover what each setting does in this chapter. There's a lot of settings! Need to find something quickly? Use the magnifying glass up top. Before looking at the settings, however, tap the avatar of the person in the upper right corner. That's going to let you add in personal information.

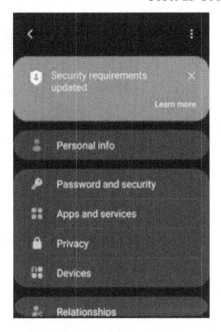

CONNECTIONS

This setting, like most settings, does exactly what it sounds like: it manages how things connect to the Internet, Bluetooth, and NFC payments (i.e. mobile credit cards).

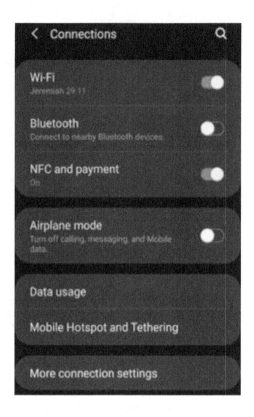

Data usage tells you how much data you've used; tapping on it gives you a deeper overview, so you can see exactly which apps used the data. Why is this important? For most, it probably won't be. I'll give an example of when it helped me: I work on the go a lot; I use the wireless on my phone to connect my laptop (which is called tethering); my MacBook was set to back up to the cloud, and little did I know it was doing this while connecting to my phone...20GB later, I was able to pinpoint what happened by looking at the data.

Below this is Hotspot and tethering. This is when you use your phone's data to connect other devices; you can use your phone's data plan, for example, to use the Internet on your iPad. Some carriers charge extra for this—mine (AT&T) includes it in the plan. To use it, tap the setting and turn it on, then name your network and password. From your other device, you find the network you set up, and connect.

Airplane mode is next. This setting turns off all wireless activity with a switch. So if you're flying and they tell you to turn everything wireless off, you can do it with a switch.

Finally, More connection settings is for doing some wireless connecting on a private network. This is not something a beginning user would need to do, and I'm not going to cover it, as the point of this book is to keep it ridiculously simple. You can also set up wireless printing and wireless emergency alerts here.

SOUNDS AND VIBRATIONS

There's a volume button on the side of your phone, so why would you need to open up a setting for it?! This setting lets you get more specific about your volume.

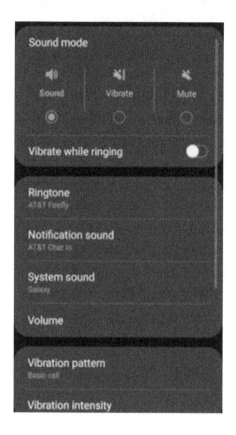

For example, you may want your alarm to ring super loud in the morning, but you want your music to play very low.

You can also use these settings to adjust the intensity of vibrations.

NOTIFICATIONS

Notifications are those pop-ups that give you alerts—like new text messages or emails. In the notification setting you can turn them off for some apps while leaving them on for others. You can also enable Do not disturb mode, which will silence all notifications.

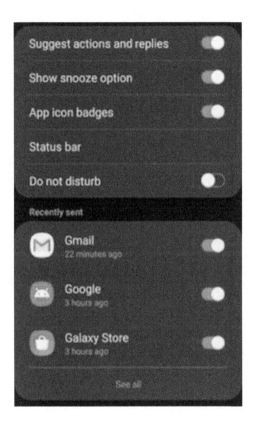

DISPLAY

As with many of the settings, almost all the main features of the Display setting can be changed outside of the app (in the notifications drop-down, for example).

This is where you'll be able to toggle on dark mode, adjust the brightness, turn on adaptive brightness, adjust the refresh rate, and toggle blue light on and off.

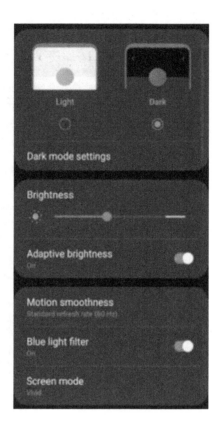

WALLPAPER / THEMES

I'm bundling these two settings together because we've talked about each of them in the section on changing your theme and wallpaper. There are no extra settings here.

HOME SCREEN

This is where you adjust your grid layout (how icons are organized and hide various apps.

LOCK SCREEN

When your phone is on standby and you lift it up: that's your lock screen. It's the screen you see before you unlock it and get to your Home screen.

The settings here change what shows up there; you can also adjust your lock setting—if, for example, you have a Face ID and want to change it to a pin ID.

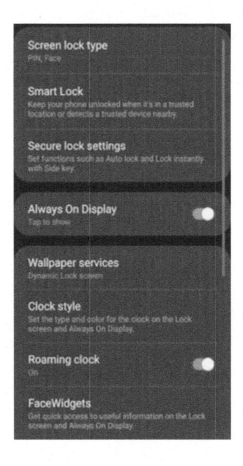

WALKING MONITOR

Do you walk and text? Your phone can tell you! Go into Digital Wellbeing, then tap on Walking monitor; not only does it track your walking time, but it tracks how often you are using your phone while walking. Watch out for that wall!

ROUTINES

Routines are what used to be known as Bixby Routines. It lets you add different modes for what you do. You can, for example, have a Work mode which has a set wallpaper and different settings; or a Sleep mode that turns off notifications.

You can access them in Settings > Modes and Routines.

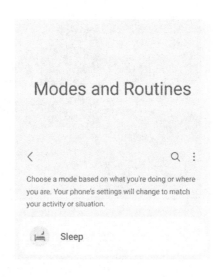

Routines is on the bottom; when you tap the tab, you'll be able to add a new routine. Routines let you add triggers for when you do things. For example, you can set a routine for When your battery level is at 5%, turn on Power saving mode.

BIXBY TEXT CALL

AI has made big enhancements, and this is clear with Bixby Text Call. This settings let's your phone answer calls for you; it's great for blocking out SPAM. To try it, you'll want to head into your call settings, then Bixby Text Call; from here you can toggle it on and off and adjust the settings.

BIOMETRICS AND SECURITY

If you want to add a fingerprint or an additional person to Face ID, you can do so in this menu. You can also update your own—if you didn't do it with glasses, for example, then go here to redo it. You can also toggle on Find My Mobile, which lets you trace where your phone is if you've misplaced it or left it behind.

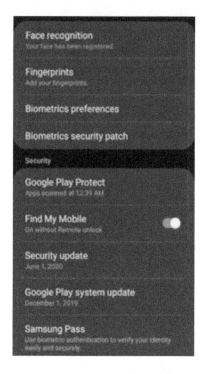

PRIVACY

Like Location Control (covered below), Privacy settings got a big upgrade in Android 10. It's so big, it now fills an entire section in the settings.

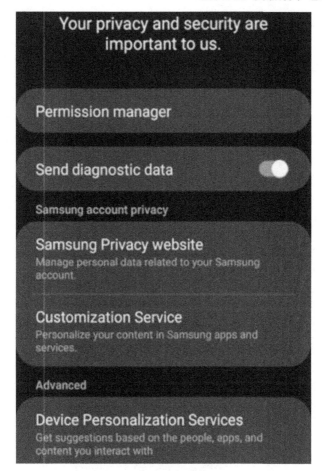

The biggest upgrade is the ability to customize what apps see what; it's no longer all or nothing. You can refine exactly how much or how little each app can see.

Tap on Permissions as one example of what you can control.

LOCATION

In the past, Location Control was an all or nothing feature—you'd decide if an app could see you all the time or none of the time. That's nice for privacy, but not nice for when you actually need someone to know your location—like when you are getting picked up by a ride app like Lyft. The new Android OS adds a new option for while you are using the app. So, for example, a ride app can only see your location while you are using the app; once the ride is over, they can no longer see what you are doing.

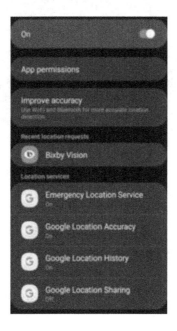

ACCOUNTS & BACKUP

If you have more than one Google account, you can tap on this to add it. If you want to remove your current account, tap on it and tap Remove—remember, however, you can have more than one account. Don't remove it just so you can add another.

You can also come here to back up your phone. It's good to do it once a month or so, but you definitely want to do it before switching to a new device.

GOOGLE

Google is where you will go to manage any Google device connected with your phone. If you are using a Google watch, for example, or a Chromecast.

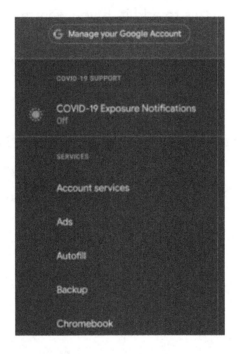

ADVANCED FEATURES

Most the features in Advanced Features are exactly what they sound: Advanced. They're features that novice users will likely never use. Things like screenshot recording features and reducing animations.

There's one important one here. One I recommend everyone use: Side key.

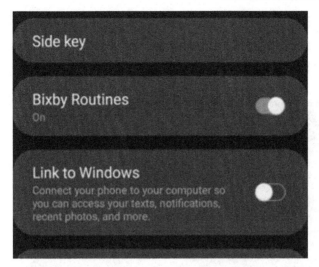

Side key is that button below the volume. Right now, if you hold it down, it goes to Bixby. Bixby isn't Samsung's most popular feature. Some people like it—many don't. If you want to change that button to power down your phone instead, then click that.

When you double tap the button, it launches the camera. You can update that too.

ADVANCED INTELLIGENCE

The first thing you'll see in Advanced Features is Advanced Intelligence—the fancy way of saying AI.

If you aren't big on AI for whatever reason, then you can go here to turn off features, or manage other settings.

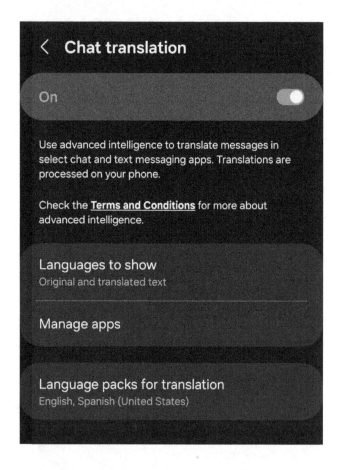

DIGITAL WELLBEING AND PARENTAL CONTROLS

Digital Wellbeing is my least favorite feature on the Samsung phone; now when my wife says, "You spend too much time on your phone"—she can actually prove it! The purpose of the setting is to help you manage your time more. It lets you know you're spending 12 hours a day updating your social media with memes of cats, and "hopefully" make you feel like perhaps you shouldn't do that.

If you have kids using your phone, this is where you can also set up parental controls.

BATTERY AND DEVICE CARE

Samsung tries to make it simple to take care of your phone. With one click (the blue Optimize now), you can have your phone scanned and any problematic apps will be closed.

You can also tap on any of the three sections: Battery, Storage, and Memory.

The battery setting is more about analytics than settings you can change. There are some settings here you can edit—you can put your phone in battery saving mode, for example. This setting is more useful if your battery is draining too quickly; it helps you troubleshoot what's going on so you can get more life from your phone.

When you first get your phone, storage won't be a big issue, but once you start taking photos (which are larger than you think) and installing apps, it's going to go very quickly.

The storage setting helps you manage this. It shows you what's taking up storage, so you can decide if you want to delete things. Just tap on any of the subsections and follow the instructions for what to do to save space.

APPS

Every app you download has different settings and permissions. A map app, for example, needs your permission to know your location. You can turn these permissions on and off here. Does it really matter? App makers can't abuse it, right? Sort of. Here's an example: a few months ago, a popular ride-sharing app made headlines because it wanted to know where passengers were after they left the ride, so they could promote different restaurants and stores and make even more money. Many felt this was both greedy and an invasion of privacy; if you are of the latter stance, then you could go in here and stop sharing your location.

How? Just tap Advanced then look at all the permissions you are giving away. Go to the permission you are concerned with and toggle the app from on to off.

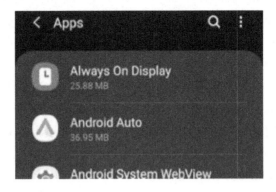

GENERAL MANAGEMENT

General management is where you go to change the language and date / time; the most important thing here, however, is Reset. This is where you can do a complete factory reset of your phone.

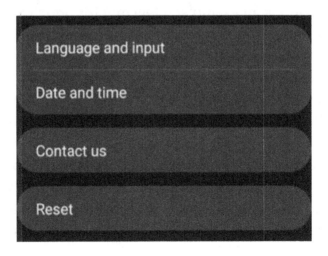

ACCESSIBILITY

Do you hate phones because the text is too small, the colors are all wrong, you can't hear anything? Or something else? That's where accessibility can help. This is where you make changes to the device to make it easier on your eyes or ears.

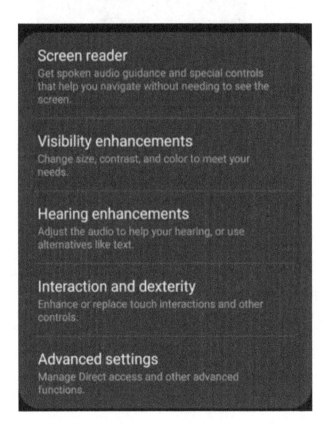

Let's dig in a little more what you will find in each of the menus.

SCREEN READER

Screen reader reads back whatever is on your phone. Push a button? It reads what that button says. Tapping the toggle will turn it on.

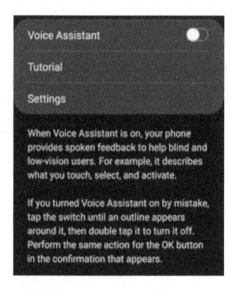

Clicking on settings will bring up settings for the voice. You can change how fast it speaks, if it speaks passwords and caller ID aloud, and more.

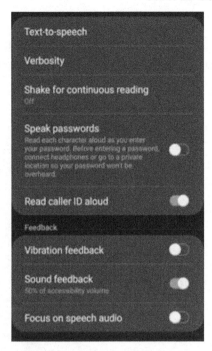

VISIBILITY ENHANCEMENTS

Visibility Enhancements changes the contrasts for people who have difficulty seeing. It also lets you change the shapes of buttons to make them stand out more.

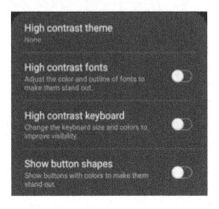

Under Size and Zoom you can turn magnification on and off; this is useful if you want apps to be larger, so you can read things without glasses.

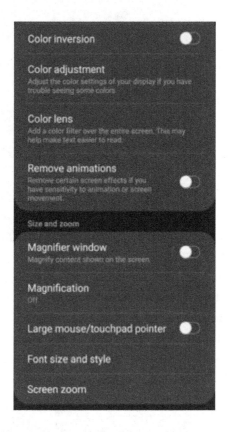

HEARING ENHANCEMENTS

Hearing enhancements is where you go to make things amplified, change to mono audio, and add hearing aid support. You can also turn on Real Time Text and Live Captioning so you can read what you might not otherwise be able to hear.

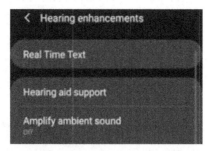

At the bottom of settings is Sound detectors, which lets you get notifications on your phone when it detects that someone has rang your door-bell or there's a baby crying.

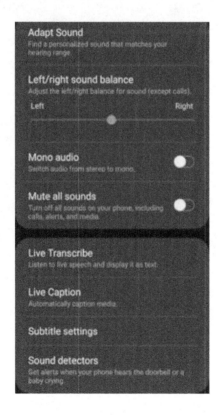

INTERACTION AND DEXTERITY

If you find that when you tap, things don't open, then Interaction and Dexterity is a setting that can help adjust the sensitivity of touch, which may make it more responsive.

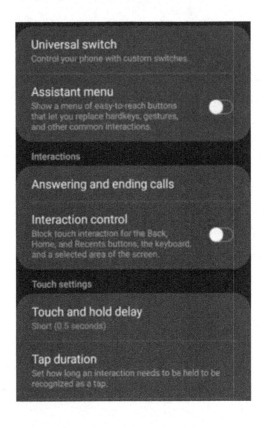

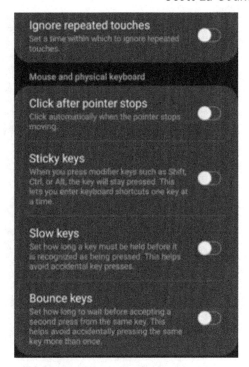

ADVANCED SETTINGS

The advance menu lets you turn your volume up / down and side button into shortcut keys. For example, you can set volume up to open an app instead of turn the volume up. You can also set up flash notifications, so your flash goes off anytime that you get an alert.

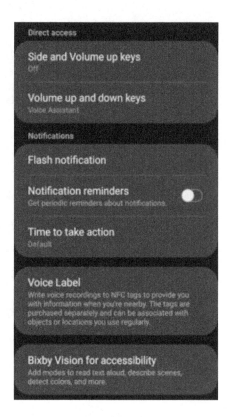

SOFTWARE UPDATE

This is where you will find general information about your phone, such as the OS you are running, the kind of phone you have, IP address, etc. It's more of an FYI, but there are a few settings here that you can change.

TIPS & SUPPORT

This isn't really a setting. It's just tips and support. You can also talk with support here.

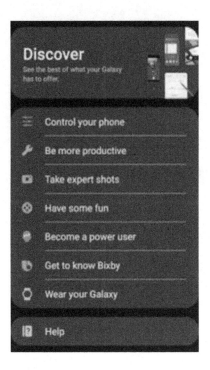

ABOUT PHONE

This is where you will find general information about your phone. Such as the OS you are running, the kind of phone you have, IP address, etc. It's more of an FYI, but there are a few settings here that you can change.

Status
View the SIM card status, IMEI, and other information.

Legal information

Software information
View the currently installed Android version, baseband version, kernel version, build number, and more.

Battery information
View your phone's battery status, remaining power, and other information.

Bonus Book: Using Gmail

Introduction

If you are like millions of people, then your first email was probably AOL, Juno, or Hotmail. Email as a communication tool, however, has been around since the 60s.

Gmail is the most widely used provider today, and if you are using it (or considering using it) there's probably a good reason: it does more than perhaps any other email provider out there.

You can make phone calls with Gmail! You can make video calls with Gmail! You can send money to friends with Gmail! There's so much you can do! But how?!

This book will show you how. It will also walk you through all the basics. So, if you've never used email in your life, then it will give you all the information you need to get started.

If you are ready to get the most out of Gmail, then let's get started!

[1]

TELL ME ABOUT ACCESSIBILITY

This chapter will cover:
- How to make Chrome easier to see, hear, and use!

ACCESSIBILITY FEATURES

We are going to do things a little backwards. Normally, I start these books with a crash course of features, but for this book, I'm going to cover accessibility features first.

Accessibility features enhance the experience for users who might have trouble seeing, hearing, or just don't know how fast the mouse pad feels.

Why?

Because there's a lot of features that might be helpful to you as you learn--such as text-to-speech.

Gmail is obviously something that you access online, which means you can use any browser you want to open it. Chrome browser? Definitely. Safari? Yep! Opera? Certainly! Any browser. So what does that mean? It means that the accessibility tools in your browser of choice will also work with Gmail.

Most browsers have a native zoom feature that makes the text bigger. It's usually found in your menu and Zoom In. As an example, below is where it is in Safari.

Chrome is very similar—under the main menu and View.

| View | History | Bookmarks | People | Windo |

Always Show Bookmarks Bar ⇧⌘B
✓ Always Show Toolbar in Full Screen ⇧⌘F
Customize Touch Bar...

Stop ⌘.
Force Reload This Page ⇧⌘R

Enter Full Screen ⌃⌘F
Actual Size ⌘0
Zoom In ⌘+
Zoom Out ⌘-

Cast...

Developer ▶

Every browser will have lots of different accessibility features. To get the most out of it, make sure you review the features on your browser of choice.

Something else that is helpful is text-to-speech. That means you can read back allowed what's on the screen. Later in this book, I'll cover how to add in apps to Gmail; there are plenty of other accessibility apps you can add in.

Personally, I don't use an add on. I use a Chrome browser plugin from TTSReader.com (you can also use it right from their website). The way this app works is anytime you want something read back, you click the button in your browser, and paste it in. I like it because it's not tied to any one software or tool. There's a free version that's add supported, or a premium version that's $9.99. There are dozens and dozens just like this app, so I encourage you to do your homework and find the best one for you.

[1]

GMAIL CRASH COURSE

This chapter will cover:
- Overview of features
- Where things are

I'm going to go quickly through this chapter. Don't worry! This is just a high-level overview. I'll slow down in future chapters to drill a little deeper into different subjects.

One thing to note: this book only covers the desktop version of Gmail; the mobile version is very much the same, but there are a few extra things—notably swipe gestures. Once you understand the desktop version, you should have no problem with the mobile app.

First things first: How do you get an email? If you already have one, great! Skip this part! In fact, you might find yourself skipping around a lot. This book is for beginning and more experienced users alike, so if you've already been using Gmail for a while, then you may jump ahead.

As a side note, you can have as many email addresses as you like—personally, I have a family one, a business one, and a bogus one (which I use to fill out forms for companies I'm not sure if I trust). So if you already have one, feel free to create another!

To get started, go to gmail.com. You'll be greeted by a very simple webpage. It's asking you to sign in. How do you sign in when you don't have an account? You don't, obviously! Just click the Create account button under the sign-in box to get started. (Note: Anytime you need to access email after you have created an email, start at this page):

Google

Sign in

to continue to Gmail

Email or phone

Forgot email?

Not your computer? Use Guest mode to sign in privately.
Learn more

Create account   Next

English (United States) ▼   Help   Privacy   Terms

When you select Create account, it's going to ask if it's for yourself or a business:

If you select business, Google's going to sell you on having a business account. That lets you use Gmail, but have your company's @ extension. Many businesses use the free personal version for their business—especially when they're just getting started.

Next, fill out the Google Account info, and hit Next:

Remember I said an account could be bogus? Here I am creating one for Jonah Simms (in case you don't know, that's the name of a fictional character on the NBC show Superstore):

Turns out I'm not the only person who is a fan of Jonah Simms—my guess is there actually is a Jonah Simms in the world. In any case, my first choice for email is gone:

You might get the same error message—with over a billion Gmail accounts out there, many usernames are taken. Just keep thinking of new ones until you find one that's not taken. I just added a number 2 to mine.

Next, Gmail will ask some more personal information about you:

Why do they want to know this? If you really want to know, click the hyperlink, and it will tell you:

Most the fields are optional. Even the gender field has an option for not saying—and one for creating a custom gender:

Privacy is big with Google. The next page has a very lengthy Terms of Service. Is creating a bogus account in violation of these terms? Feel free to read this lengthy legal document to find out!

Or be like everyone else and scroll until the end and hit I agree:

Congrats! You now have email!

When you hit Next, Gmail will ask what kind of view you want. There are three. The first is the default view that most people select:

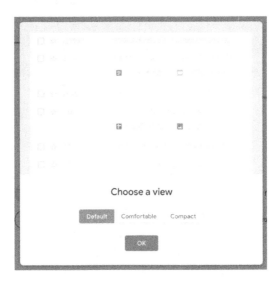

It's simple and it shows attachments—by that, I mean you can open attachments without opening the email.

Next is Comfortable; it's a little simpler. That open attachment option is gone and you'll see instead a paperclip next to emails with attachments:

The last option is Compact. This is very similar to the Comfortable theme, but it's more compressed so you can see more emails on your screen. None work better than the other—it's just a preference (one that can be changed). When you have picked the one you want, select OK:

You'll now have access to all of your email—it's going to be empty right now, obviously:

The menu on the left side is the one you'll use the most. Very quickly (again, we'll cover this more later), you'll see your main Inbox, Starred mail (this means you've basically flagged email to go in a special area), Snoozed (email that will return to your email at a later date), Sent, Drafts (if you accidently close an email before its sent, it will go here), and finally, More:

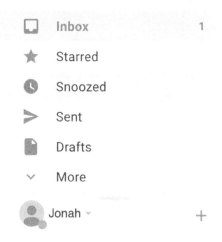

Selecting More brings up a larger menu. The thing you'll use the most here is probably Spam and Trash (where deleted emails go). Why would you use Spam? It's not uncommon for important emails to go here. It's a good idea to check it every day or every other day. If you aren't entering contests 24/7, then you shouldn't get a lot of Spam:

- Important
- Chats
- Scheduled
- All Mail
- Spam
- Trash
- ▸ **Categories**
- Manage labels
- + Create new label

Above this menu is the Compose button; you'll click that to start a new email:

Next to Compose is a button with three lines. That expands and collapses your menu. Click it

once and watch it collapse and become more nar-
row. Click it again and it goes back to normal:

Below the menu is a dialog box with a quota-
tion. That's where you go to start a Hangout (a
Hangout is like a video call—another free service
from Google), or chat with someone:

To the right of Hangouts, you can see how much space you've used. Unless you send a lot of attachments, you'll probably never exceed it. If you do, you can buy more space very cheaply. As of this writing, you can get 100 GB for 20 bucks a year.

To the far, lower right, you can see your account activity. This tells you all the sessions that are signed in. Let's say you went to a public library and forgot to sign out. Yikes, right?! Go here and just click Details:

If there's a remote session in place—meaning someone is using your account from a distant place, then there's going to be an option to sign out. And speaking of signing out—how do you do that?! Go to the upper right corner. If you have a profile picture, then it will show your beautiful face. If not, it will have your abbreviation. When you click on that, you can Sign out:

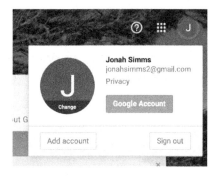

Next to that is a button with nine dots. Click that and you'll see some of Google's most popular apps. Since you have gmail, you have access to all of them:

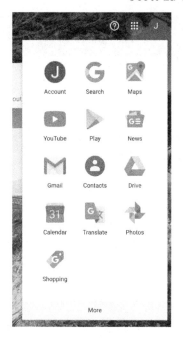

Just below that, you'll see a configure button. This is where you can do things like change the theme we set up earlier. We are going to spend a lot of time in this area. For now, just know where it is:

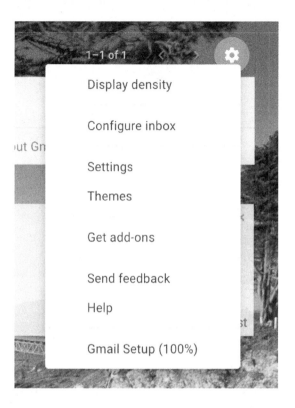

On the right side is the side menu. Here, you can get to your calendar, your idea book, your tasks, or you can add Gmail plugin apps (i.e. third party apps that tie into Gmail):

Finally, at the top is the search menu. This is where you can search your mail:

Near the bottom of your inbox, you'll see a 10% setup progress. What does that mean? You have email! Aren't you all setup?! Technically, yes. This is Google's way of helping you learn the email ropes. It actually is helpful, and you can do it very quickly.

The first option is theme:

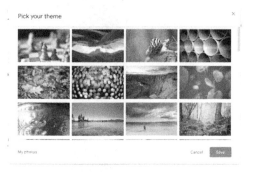

Theme puts an image on your inbox to make it a little more personal. Go ahead and pick one! Even if you haven't hit save yet, you'll see a preview:

There are a few options on the bottom to help make the image easier to see behind your email. The first (the A button) makes the email area either dark or light. (You can change all of this later!)

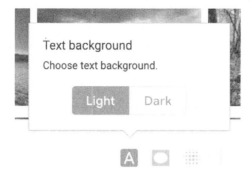

When you toggle it, you'll notice the background of your email is changing:

Next is vignette, which just makes the corners of the image darker. Sliding it to the right will adjust the darkness:

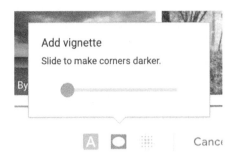

Finally, you can apply a blur. Personally, I like this feature best; when you have a really sharp image, it can make it harder to see text on the screen. Blurring the image makes emails and text stand out more, in my opinion.

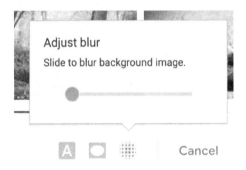

Once you hit save, you'll notice that this event is not done. You are one step closer to completing Gmail's quick setup!

The next option is Learn how to use Gmail. Click on that and it brings up a help box. I do recommend spending a few seconds here. It has some good tips.

Close it and the activity is done!

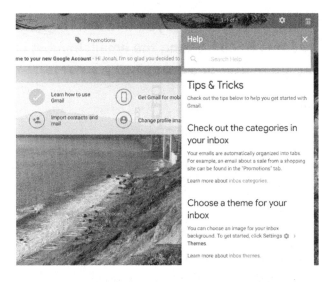

If you already have an email (such as a work email) and you want to import over all the contacts, click the Import contacts option; if you just want this to show that you've completed the setup, then click it and then cancel it:

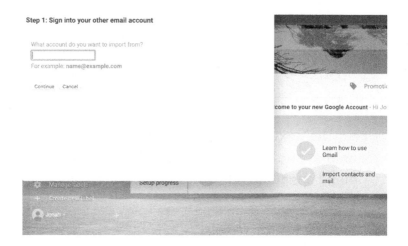

This is going to walk you through the quick and easy steps to connecting the email. In most cases, it's just a matter of signing into your email:

Sign in

to continue to Gmail ShuttleCloud Migration

Getting the mobile app is next. The mobile app lets you read email on your phone or tablet—you can also get a mobile-friendly version of Gmail by going to Gmail.com from your browser. Using a native app, however, let's you get notifications of new mail in real time:

Next, select a profile photo. This is what people see when they get a message from you. You don't have to pick one, but I do recommend it. Sometimes people don't know who you are until they see your face:

Once you complete that, you'll get the 100% badge of honor!

[2]

HOW TO SEND AND RECEIVE MAIL

This chapter will cover:
- Sending email
- Adding attachments
- Reading email
- Adding labels
- Adding contacts
- Searching for email

HOW TO SEND EMAIL

Now that you know your way around, let's have some fun and send an email.

Email comes naturally for most people. But there's more inside the email then just compose and send. There's a lot of extra formatting you can do.

In case this is your first time using Gmail, or your first time using email, click the Compose button on the upper left hand side:

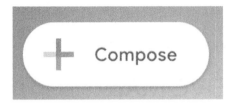

This opens up the New Message window:

Click the arrow next to the X in the upper left corner. That makes the message larger; click it again to return to normal size:

By default, all you see is the "To" field. Enter someone's email here; if you want to send a CC or BCC, then click the button that says CC or BCC:

Cc Bcc

CC is a carbon copy—a copy of the email that will go to a person that you think needs to see the email, but does not necessarily need to reply. A BCC is a blind carbon copy. This means other people cannot see who you sent it to. If you are sending a huge list, one hack is to send it to yourself and BCC everyone else. This way everyone gets what you are sending, but they can't see everyone else on the list.

To

Cc |

Bcc

Subject

When you start typing in the body, you'll see the format bar. If you don't see it hit the A next to Send. You can add emojis to the subject, but you can't change the formatting here—for example, you can't Bold the subject.

The non-format menu is at the bottom of the message. I already said what "A" does. The paperclip attaches a file, the one next to that inserts a link into the message (you can also highlight a word and do CTRL+K for this), the face inserts an emoji, the triangle is Google Drive (if you have a file you want to attach that's in Google Drive versus your computer), next to that is to insert a picture, and finally, the little button with the clock puts the email in confidential mode.

Confidential mode is James Bond for email! This message will self-destruct kind of stuff! It takes away the ability for the person to forward, print, or copy the message. You can also set limits on when it expires, and require a code.

Confidential mode

Recipients won't have the option to forward, copy, print, or download this email. Learn more

SET EXPIRATION

Expires in 1 week   ▾   Fri, Aug 16, 2019

REQUIRE PASSCODE
All passcodes will be generated by Google. ⑦

◉ No SMS passcode   ○ SMS passcode

Cancel   Save

Finally, the money key lets you either send money via email or ask for money. You just need to add a debit card. It's kind of like Google's version of PayPal, but without the fees:

The three dots in the bottom left corner opens up the email menu; this lets you do things like spell

check and print. You can also add a label, which we'll cover more in the next section.

Finally, the trash icon deletes the message:

If you accidently close the message (or if you do it on purpose), go to that side menu and select Drafts. It will be there waiting for you. Just click it and the email will reopen.

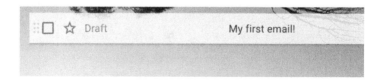

When you are ready to send the email, click the blue Send. If you want to schedule it (so it sends later), then just hit the arrow next to it:

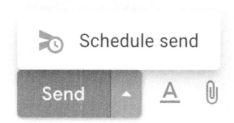

Google will show you common times to schedule it:

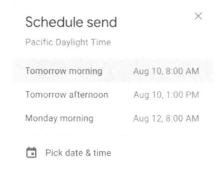

If those times don't work, then select Pick date & time, which opens up a calendar:

Pick date & time

August 2019				‹	›		Aug 9, 2019
S	M	T	W	T	F	S	
28	29	30	31	1	2	3	9:29 PM
4	5	6	7	8	9	10	
11	12	13	14	15	16	17	
18	19	20	21	22	23	24	
25	26	27	28	29	30	31	
1	2	3	4	5	6	7	

Cancel   Schedule send

HOW TO READ EMAIL

A lot of people get an email, open an email, and reply to email. Sound familiar? There's so much more you can do to organize your inbox and be more productive.

The inbox is that big area in the middle of your screen. If you just started, then you probably have an email from Andy from Google:

Above that are three tabs: Primary (where most of your email is), Social (friend requests and things pertaining to social networks), and Promotions (offers from companies you subscribe to). If someone swears up and down that they sent you an email and you don't see it in your Primary tab, then check Spam (in the menu to your left) or one of those tabs:

Not a fan of tabs and want to get rid of them? Or you are a fan and you want more? We are going to cover this soon when we talk about settings, but for now, click on Social. Near the bottom of your screen there's a message about the tab being empty, and how you can add or remove the tab. Click that blue inbox settings button:

Your Social tab is empty.

Emails from social networks, media-sharing sites, dating services and other social sites will be shown here.

To add or remove tabs click inbox settings.

You'll notice there are three tabs with checkmarks. Those are your active tabs. You cannot uncheck primary, but you can check or uncheck anything else. Once you make your selection, hit the Save button:

Select tabs to enable   ×

☑ Primary   Choose which message categories to show as inbox
                   tabs. Other messages will appear in the Primary tab.
☑ Social
                   Deselect all categories to go back to your old inbox
☑ Promotions

☐ Updates

☐ Forums

Starred messages

☑ Include starred in
   Primary

                                        Cancel   Save

Click anywhere on the email you want to open.
The top portion of the email is your main menu.
The first button (the arrow) will get you back to
your inbox; you can also get there by clicking on
the Inbox link on the left menu. These menu options are also available in your Inbox when you click
the check box on any of the messages:

← 🗀 ❗ 🗑 📧 🕐 🗂 📦 ⋮

The first three buttons on the menu are the
email options. Let's say you've read the email—
now what? You can either archive it (the down-ar-
row button), report it as junk (the ! button), or delete it (the trashcan button). If you don't do any of
these three things, then the email will remain in
your inbox. If you archive it, it will go to the folder
marked All Mail—it will no longer show in your inbox. If you mark it as junk, then it goes in the
folder marked Spam, which is eventually emptied
automatically if you don't do it. If you delete it, it

goes to your Trash folder, but, like Spam mail, it's not gone for good. You have thirty days to remove it.

If you accidently delete something or mark it as Spam, then go to the folder (either Spam or Trash), check the box next to the email, and select the button with the folder and right arrow:

Once you press that, it will ask you where you want to move the email to:

When you return to your inbox, you'll notice that the email is no longer bold. That's because it's been read. If you select the button with the mail symbol on it, it will mark it as unread. If you press the button with the clock, it will snooze it. Snooze means it will move it out of your inbox for a set period of time, and then move it back in at its designated time. I use this feature a lot for reservations and appointments. I schedule those emails to move back into the inbox on the day of the event, so it's easy to find. If you snoozed a message, but want to unsnoozed it, just go into the Snooze folder and follow the steps above for moving trash back into the inbox.

You already learned what the next button does—it moves the mail to another folder. Just like you can move trash or junk back into your inbox, you can also add new mail into another folder. The last button is the Label button:

ADDING LABELS

When you click the label button, it shows you all the labels already created. If you want to create a new one select Create New (you can also go into Manage Labels to edit or delete one that you have already created):

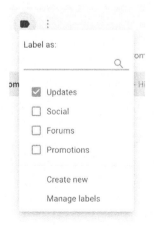

Next, enter the name. There's an option to "Nest a label under:" This doesn't work until you have created at least one custom label (those four that Google created don't count).

New label   ×

Please enter a new label name:

My First Label

☐ Nest label under:

Cancel   Create

Once it's created, return to your inbox and you'll see the email now has the label name next to it:

☑ ☆ **Andy from Google**   My First Label **Jonah, welco...**

You can see all messages with that label by clicking on the label from the left menu:

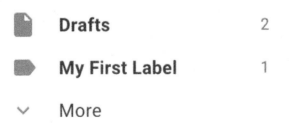

📄 **Drafts**   2

🏷 **My First Label**   1

˅ More

MORE EMAIL OPTIONS

At the end of the menu is the button with three dots. This brings up some of the less commonly used features. We will cover most of them later in the book:

The 1 of 1 (it varies depending on the number of emails you have) with the arrow keys lets you go through emails without going back to the inbox. The right arrow takes you to the next email and the left goes back to the previous:

1 of 1   ‹   ›

The keyboard changes the language of the email. This is helpful if you are replying to an email in another language. Click Input Tools Settings and you'll see dozens of different languages:

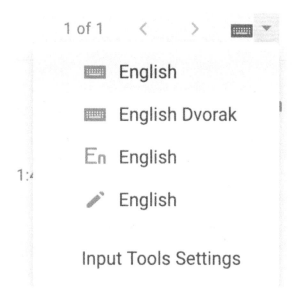

The Configure button will be discussed as we get to each of these features:

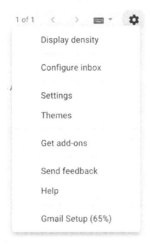

In the body of the email itself, there are a few things to note. First, if you hover over the sender's name, you can add them to your contacts, set up a calendar event with them, or email them a separate email:

On the right side of the message, there are several things you should note. The first is the time; this tells you when an email arrived (not when you opened it):

11:44 AM (6 hours ago)

Next to that is the star. By default, all emails have no star. Stars help you organize your mail, and make important emails stand out. You can have a folder with 100 emails, and filter it by only Starred emails (which you should have less of).

Next to the star is the reply button:

And next to the reply is a button with three dots. This gives you a long list of different options—most you will never use:

At the bottom of the email are two additional buttons: to Reply or Forward the message:

When you reply, it looks just like composing an email, but the person's name and the subject is already there, and the email is at the bottom of the original message—not like a popup box (as it is when you compose a new message):

Forward looks similar, but there's a place to type in a recipient under "To":

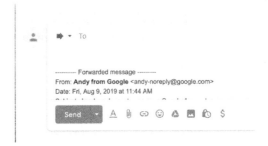

ADDING CONTACTS

Now you are ready to email someone new. Go over to the side to your contacts. Where is it? Exactly! Gmail doesn't have a dedicated place for contacts in the app. When you type someone's name, it will predict what you are typing and pull the contact up. But how do you add a contact?

You have to go to a separate website: contacts.google.com. Here you can import, export, and lots of other things. We'll be focusing on the most important thing: adding a contact:

Click the Create contact button:

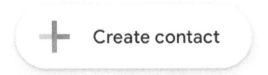

This gives you several things you can add:

Create new contact

| First name | Last name | ⊗ |
| Company | Job title | ⊗ |
| Email |
| Phone |
| Notes |

More fields   Cancel   Save

Not comprehensive enough?! Click More fields:

I'm going to add one for my very good friend with an unfortunate name: John Doe. I can create a label for him so I know if he's a work friend or family member:

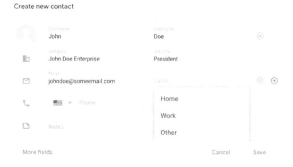

Once I save it and click his name from my contact list, it displaces everything you have inputted about good old John. You can even click on his email (I used Andy's from Google for this example) and it will open the email right up:

SEARCHING MAIL

Finding email is pretty easy with Google. You can simply search for a keyword like "budget":

Or you can click the arrow next to the search box and have more details. You can search for the word "Budget" but tell Gmail that you only want to see emails from a certain person, sent on a certain date, and it included an attachment:

Q Search mail

From		
To		
Subject		
Has the words		
Doesn't have		
Size	greater than ▾	MB ▾
Date within	1 day ▾	📅
Search	All Mail	▾

☐ Has attachment   ☐ Don't include chats

Create filter   **Search**

[3]

CHATS AND PHONE / VIDEO CALLS

This chapter will cover:
- Chat messing in Gmail
- Making / receiving calls in Gmail
- Google Hangouts

Email is cool, but today people are all about real-time answers. That's where Google Chat and Hangouts become important.

These tools are both in the same place. Chat is like an instant message and Hangouts is a video call. To get started with either, go to Start a new one below the conversations icon:

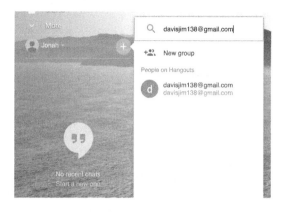

After your first Hangout, it will show you've had a conversation already:

To start a new one, just click the + sign as in the image below:

You can also bring this up with the menu bar on the very bottom left side of your screen. Here, I'll point out one icon you should know: the phone:

When you click that, you can make a free phone call right from your browser! There's not a lot to it, so I won't cover it in detail. Add the number you want and hit enter. That's it! When a person gets the call, it will say unknown. If you want your own personal Google number, then hit the + next to the $0.00. It will walk you through the steps to get a number. Why does it say $0.00 if it's free? Because it's only free within the U.S. and Canada. If you call outside that, there is a cost—albeit a low one. Some countries cost $0.01 a minute, some more remote, undeveloped countries cost over $1 a minute.

Back to Chat/Hangout; once you type in a valid email, it will open a box where you can begin the conversation. The person on the other end sees something similar. Type your message where it says Send a message, and hit enter/return:

Want to do a group chat? Click the icon of a person with a +, then add the person's email:

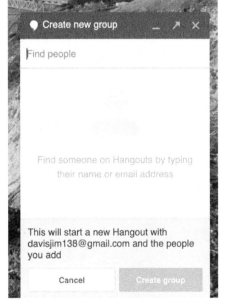

The configure button has several options such as if you want to archive or delete the conversation (if you delete it, then you won't be able to recover it):

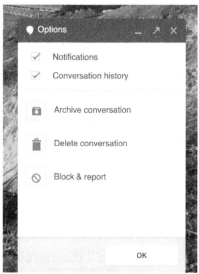

To start a Hangout, click the camera button. This opens a separate window. If it's your first Hangout, it's going to ask for a few permissions. Basically, Google is asking your computer if it's okay to use your webcam and mic:

As you're getting set up, the other person will see a notification in Gmail saying someone wants to video call them:

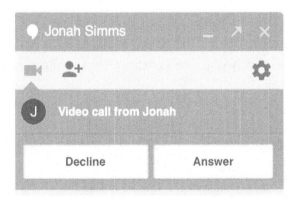

If you didn't set up your camera or mic, you can still do it while you are on the call. Just click the configure button in the upper right corner.

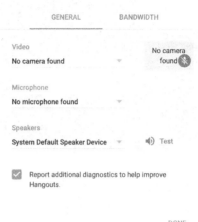

In the bottom left corner, there's an option to send messages. This is like the Chat we just saw. It's helpful if you are sending links while you are on the call:

In the upper right corner, you'll see three dots; this brings up the Hangouts option. These are pretty self-explanatory, but one in particular that you should know about: Share screen. Share screen lets the person on the other end see what's on your screen. This is very helpful when you are troubleshooting a problem with someone.

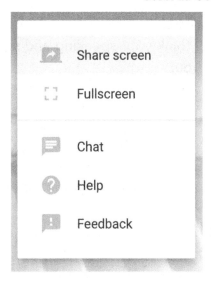

If you want to invite someone else into the hangout and have a group call, click on the person icon. It's similar to adding someone to a group text. Just add their email. You can also copy a link to the Hangout and share it. Anyone with the link can get in after you approve them.

Finally, on the middle of the screen is where you go to hang up; in this section, you can also turn off your Mic or Webcam. If you are in a group Hangout, it's best to leave your mic off when you aren't speaking. It often picks up noises and Google will think your speaking and switch the camera to you.

[4]

SETTINGS

This chapter will cover:
- Changing default settings
- Configuring your inbox to fit your needs
- Adding email signature

Settings is where you go to customize your Inbox even more. We've already covered several things found here; I'll quickly reference it again where applicable.

Because this is a simple guide, I'm going to skim over some of the more advanced features that you probably won't be using; I'll cover them in case it's a topic you want to further investigate later.

To get started, click the configuration button on the righthand side of your email:

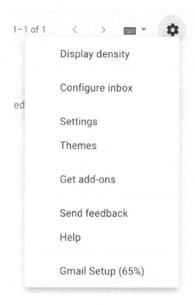

Display density was one of the first things covered in this book. This is how your inbox looks—compact with attachments not shown, for example:

Configure inbox is where you turn those tabs on and off:

Select tabs to enable ×

☑ Primary
☐ Social
☑ Promotions
☐ Updates
☐ Forums

Choose which message categories to show as inbox tabs. Other messages will appear in the Primary tab.

Deselect all categories to go back to your old inbox.

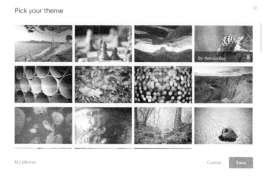

Starred messages

☑ Include starred in Primary

Cancel **Save**

Skipping down a little, Themes is where you pick the background for your inbox:

Pick your theme ×

My photos Cancel **Save**

Gmail setup is that little bar we saw on the bottom of our screen when we first started Gmail; mine went back to 65% because I merely opened the setting, but didn't change it. It doesn't really matter—Gmail doesn't behave differently because you are not at 100%.

Settings is where we will spend the biggest chunk of our time in this chapter. When you click Settings, you'll see a menu at the top of your Inbox with a lot of options.

Let's start with the first menu: General. This is where you'll change things like the language and the style of your emails. There's a lot here you will not use. We'll look at some of the things you might use.

Default text style is the font, font size, and font color you use in your email. Let's say you love the color red and want big fonts. You could manually change this for every email you send, but you can also make the change here and every email you send will have that style.

Default text style:
(Use the 'Remove formatting' button
on the toolbar to reset the default
text style)

Sans Serif ▾ ⊤T ▾ A ▾ ✗
This is what your body text will look like.

Conversation View is on by default. It groups all similar email topics together and makes it easy to follow conversations; if you aren't a fan, then turn it off here:

Conversation View:
(sets whether emails of the same
topic are grouped together)

◉ **Conversation view on**
○ **Conversation view off**

Nudges is also on by default. If an email needs a reply and you haven't done it, Nudges will automatically move it to the top of your inbox after a set number of days:

Nudges:
Learn more

☑ **Suggest emails to reply to** - Emails you might have forgotten to respond to will appear at the top of your inbox
☑ **Suggest emails to follow up on** - Sent emails you might need to follow up on will appear at the top of your inbox

Smart reply is a somewhat new feature. A Google bot gives you a reply that it thinks is appropriate. So let's say someone emails you, "Here's the doc that you wanted." The suggested reply would probably be, "Thanks!" It would show the text in grey, and hitting the tab button will add it:

Smart Reply:
(Show suggested replies when
available.)

◉ **Smart Reply on**
○ **Smart Reply off**

Desktop notifications allows Gmail to send you alerts on your desktop/laptop saying that you have a new email or other notification:

Desktop notifications:
(allows Gmail to display popup notifications on your desktop when new email messages arrive)
Learn more

Click here to enable desktop notifications for Gmail.
New mail notifications on - Notify me when any new message arrives in my inbox or primary tab
Important mail notifications on - Notify me only when an important message arrives in my inbox
◉ **Mail notifications off**

Signature is how you sign off on emails. That way if you always sign off:

Sincerely,
John Doe
111-111-1111

you could add that signature here, and every email would include it. You only see the signature after you send the email.

Vacation responder can automatically reply to emails saying you are away and won't be able to respond. You have to set the first day, but the last day is optional. If you don't set the last day, then make sure you come back in and turn it off when you are done with your vacation:

At the bottom is the Save Changes/Cancel button; if it's greyed out, then no changes have been made. Note: some of these menus have the save options and others save automatically—make sure and look at the bottom before closing the menu.

Save Changes   Cancel

Click on any word on the menu bar and it brings up a new menu. The next one is Labels. We've already covered this section, but this is how you get back to it.

General   Labels   Inbox   Accounts and Import   Filters and Blocked Addresses   Forwarding and POP/IMAP   Add

Themes

System labels	Show in label list	
Inbox		
Starred	**show** hide	
Snoozed	**show** hide	
Important	show **hide**	
Chats	show **hide**	
Sent	**show** hide	
Scheduled	show hide **show if unread**	
Drafts	**show** hide show if unread	
All Mail	show **hide**	
Spam	show **hide** show if unread	
Trash	show **hide**	

Categories	Show in label list	Show in message list
Categories	show **hide**	
Social	show **hide**	show **hide**
Updates	show **hide**	show **hide**
Forums	show **hide**	show **hide**

If you created a label earlier, then you should
see it at the bottom of this setting:

Labels	Show in label list	Show in message list	Actions
Create new label			
My First Label	**show** hide show if unread	**show** hide	remove edit
1 conversation			

Note: Removing a label will not remove the messages with that label.

We've also seen many of the settings in the Inbox already.

There is a setting at the bottom that changes the order of emails, for example, if you want to show unread first. That means you may have a newer email that you've already read that will be lower than an Unread one (or whatever you have selected):

Accounts and Import is where you can go to change your email:

You can also change the name that you send mail as. So if you send mail as Jonah Simms, but want to send it instead as J Simms, then just click edit info on the right-hand side:

Send mail as:
(Use Gmail to send from your other email addresses)
Learn more
Jonah Simms <jonahsimms2@gmail.com>
Add another email address
edit info

You can also add another email account in this setting. Just click Add a mail account. Why would you do this? Personally, I have several email accounts, and I have all mail forwarded to the main one. When I add other accounts, I can reply to them from my main account. So I have several accounts, but I never log into them. I have one for professional contacts; one for giveaways; one for family and friends.

Check mail from other accounts: Add a mail account
Learn more

Using Gmail for work?   Businesses get yourname@c

Filters and Blocked Addresses is where you go if there's someone you never want to speak to. You will still get messages from them, but they will go to your Spam. If the friend gets on your good side again, just go back and uncheck them.

General Labels Inbox Accounts and Import Filters and Blocked Addresses Forwarding and

Themes

The following filters are applied to all incoming mail:

Select: All, None

Export   Delete

Create a new filter Import filters

The following email addresses are blocked. Messages from these addresses will appear in Spam:

You currently have no blocked addresses.

Select: All, None

Forwarding and POP/IMAP get pretty technical. If you want to add a work email to Gmail, you can do it here, but you will probably need the IT guy's help in getting some of the settings. One thing you should know here is Forwarding. Forwarding lets you forward all of your email to another inbox. So let's say you want to give people another email so they don't know your main one; their email gets forwarded to your main one, so you don't have to keep checking this one.

General Labels Inbox Accounts and Import Filters and Blocked Addresses Forwarding and POP/IMAP Add-ons

Themes

Forwarding:
Learn more

Add a forwarding address

Tip: You can also forward only some of your mail by creating a filter!

POP download:
Learn more

1. Status: POP is disabled
   Enable POP for **all mail**
   Enable POP for **mail that arrives from now on**

2. When messages are accessed with POP keep Gmail's copy in the inbox

3. Configure your email client (e.g. Outlook, Eudora, Netscape Mail)
   Configuration instructions

IMAP access:
(access Gmail from other clients using IMAP)
Learn more

Status: IMAP is disabled
  Enable IMAP
  ○ Disable IMAP

Configure your email client (e.g. Outlook, Thunderbird, iPhone)
Configuration instructions

Save Changes   Cancel

Add-ons will be covered in the next chapter. This is where you can add third-party apps:

General Labels Inbox Accounts and Import Filters and Blocked Addresses Forwarding and POP/IMAP Add-ons

Themes

Add-ons:
Learn more

Get add-ons
Add-ons are applications that extend the functionality of Gmail.

  Enable developer add-ons for my account

Chat is pretty straight forward. It turns the chat widget on the left side on and off:

Advanced isn't as advanced as it sounds. By default, everything is disabled. If you want something turned on, just click Enable:

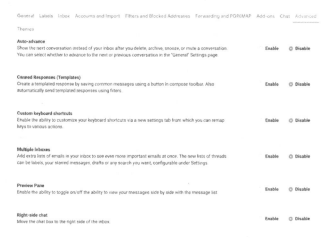

Finally, Offline lets you download your email to your computer:

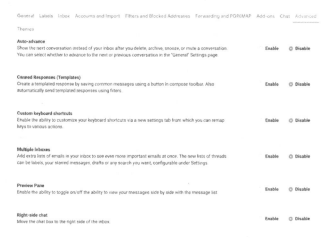

When you are ready to sign off for the day, click your profile photo or name in the upper right corner:

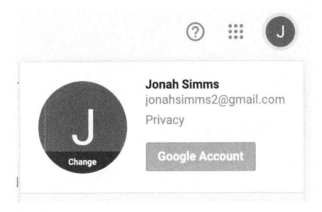

In addition to signing off, this is also where you can add additional accounts. So you can be signed in to multiple accounts and toggle between them.

[5]

CALENDAR

This chapter will cover:
- How to find your calendar
- Changing views
- Adding events
- Inviting people to events

The point of this book is to show you how to use your Gmail account; because a lot of your email is tied to the calendar, I'll give a very high-level overview of Google Calendar here. To get started, go to calendar.google.com. By default, it will give you a monthly view of your calendar:

You can switch from monthly/yearly/daily or any other views by clicking on Week over on the side; you can also go to the following months (or previous months) by clicking on the arrows next to the smaller calendar.

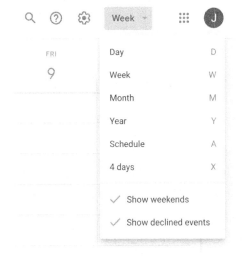

Over on the left side, just above "Holidays in the United States" is the option to add other calendars. For example, your spouse or sibling may have a calendar; they can share it with you so you can arrange appointments. This is frequently used in business when a manager needs to see an employee—they'll share their calendar and tell the employee to find an opening and create an event.

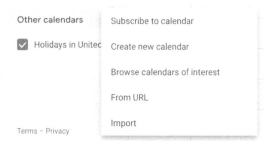

So how do you create an event? Click the big Create button over on the left side:

This brings up a small box that will ask you for the details. You can create it as a traditional event, or also as just a reminder or a task. You can also add a location and guests. If you add guests, they will need to accept your invitation:

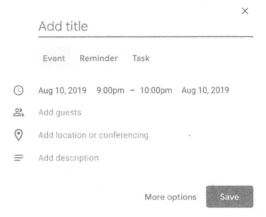

Clicking on More options, expands the box to show you even more things to add. This is what you would use if you want to attach something to the event (like the meeting minutes). You can also set up notifications, so you'll get an alert at a set time saying that the meeting is beginning.

[6]

THIRD PARTY APPS

This chapter will cover:
- What are third party apps
- How to find / add third party apps
- How to remove third party apps

There are hundreds and hundreds of third party apps for Gmail. In this book, I'm not going to cover the apps you should have. It's really a preference. I'm going to cover what they are in general and how to add them.

So what are they? Think of them like Add-ons. Dropbox (the cloud-based file locker), for example, has a third-party app that puts a Dropbox icon in your message box. You know when you are composing a message and you see that paperclip to attach a file? You'll also see a Dropbox icon to attach a file in Dropbox.

As I mentioned earlier, this is where you can go to find accessibility apps for Gmail.

On the right side menu, click the + button:

This brings up a box that shows you all the possible apps you can add to Gmail (use at your own risk!); the first ones you see are the more popular apps:

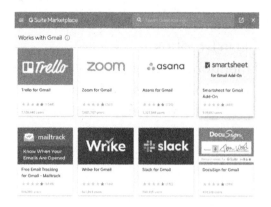

If you click the three lines in the upper left side, this lets you see all the different categories.

At the very bottom of the list is the Manage Apps option; that lets you remove or control the apps that you have already added:

[7]

HOW TO CANCEL GMAIL

This chapter will cover:
- Do you need to cancel Gmail?
- How to cancel Gmail

Now that you've read all of this, what if you decide Gmail isn't for you? You have two options:
1. Don't log back in.
2. Manually delete it.

There's usually not a direct reason to delete your account. If you are worried someone will hack into something you never use, then that would be a reason—but Google, being Google, invests a lot of money into security.

The advantage of keeping it is you always have access to emails if you ever need them. Maybe one day you'll need something you never imagined you would need.

If you want to delete your account permanently, then head over here—and remember! There's no recovering email once you delete it, so be extra sure before you do this:

https://myaccount.google.com

Email has settings and your account has settings as well. This is sort of your master settings. It controls all Google Apps tied to your account:

From here, go to Data & personalization:

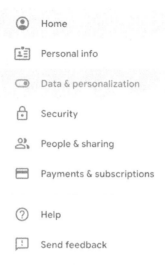

There is a lot here. Scroll down a bit until you get to Download, delete, or make a plan for your data. Next, click Delete a service or your account:

You can delete everything, or you can delete one service in particular—so if you have a YouTube and Gmail account, but only want to delete the Gmail account, then you'd choose service. If you want to go nuclear and delete everything, then delete your Google Account:

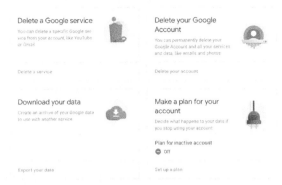

I only have a Gmail account tied to this account, so when I try to delete a service, all I see is Gmail. To delete it, hit the trashcan next to it. Do so at your own risk! This will delete your email and you'll never be able to recover it again!

← Delete a Google service

A Google Account offers many services. Some of these services can be deleted from your account individually.

Consider downloading your data before deleting a service.

DOWNLOAD DATA

Or choose a service below:

M Gmail
1 conversation

That's it! Gmail in a nutshell! I hope you'll be able to use email in ways you didn't know was possible.

INDEX

ABOUT THE AUTHOR

Scott La Counte is a UX Designer and writer. His first book, *Quiet, Please: Dispatches from a Public Librarian* (Da Capo 2008) was the editor's choice for the Chicago Tribune and a Discovery title for the Los Angeles Times.

He has written dozens of best-selling how-to guides on tech products.

He teaches UX Design at UC Berkeley.

You can connect with him at ScottDouglas.org.

Made in the USA
Las Vegas, NV
14 December 2024

14218092R00184